Cozy Country

DECORATING

Cozy Country

Decorating

FABRIC IDEAS FOR THE HOME

Adele Corcoran & Carol Hart

Project designs & illustrations by Anny Evason

MUSEUM QUILTS

Published by Museum Quilts (UK) Inc.
254-258 Goswell Road, London EC1V 7EB

Copyright © Museum Quilts Publications, Inc. 1997

Text © Adele Corcoran and Carol Hart 1997
Illustrations © Anny Evason 1997
Project designs © Anny Evason 1997
Photography © David Johnson 1997
Monogram lettering on page 131 taken from *Patterns for Cake Decorating* published by Merehurst Limited

Editors: Ljiljana Ortolja-Baird and Simona Hill
Designer: Kit Johnson

A CIP catalogue record for this book is available from the British Library

ISBN: 1-897954-37-9

Origination by Interscan Graphics, Malaysia
Printed and bound by Star Standard Industries, Singapore

Contents

INTRODUCTION

Draped, hung or used in accents in cushions, quilts, tablecloths and wallhangings, fabric softens the hard edges of our homes and creates a warmer and friendlier environment. Crisp cottons in muted tones are essential to a country cottage, while warm, thick wools in rich, saturated colors bring warmth and a cozy glow.

Color too can change our mood and lift our spirits. Clear, sky blue with golden yellow, mauve and hints of white remind us of spring days, a welcome blessing after the bright Christmas reds and deep bottle greens. Pastel pinks, soft reds, leafy greens, lilac, lavender, and orange herald summer, adding a light, fresh touch to our rooms; and hot red, russet, golden brown, burnt orange, deep purple and crimson summon the harvest fields of fall. Used as a single, bold shade or in multi-colored patterns, color offers exciting design and decorating possibilities.

Cultures from every part of the globe use fabric, texture and color for practical, functional purposes – to keep out the heat, to keep out the cold – and for decoration, to embellish, adorn, and add the finishing touches to our homes. Borne of necessity the way we use fabric has shaped our cultural identity. With thrift and economy old clothes were recycled to make rag rugs to cover the cold flags of an old cottage. Strong splashes of color create drama and interest in a contemporary, minimalist environment as well as in a sparse white-washed Welsh cottage. Middle Eastern nations adorn their living spaces with rich fabrics in opulent, jewel-like colors. Victorian England stuffed its parlors with sumptuous velvets and brocades; the Balkan people surround themselves with layers of richly embroidered domestic linen. Textiles are not only a source of keeping out the cold but help enrich our lives.

Fabrics come in an exciting variety of textures, weights and colors. For the projects in this book we have chosen to use just a few from the huge selection of readily-available natural fabrics – cotton, corduroy, wool, flannel and felt – these fabrics take dye well, producing saturated, solid colors, and are easy to work with. The newly available washable felt means it is now possible to use this non-woven material for more than just children's toys and projects. Authors Adele Corcoran and Carol Hart have made innovative use of these fabrics in this book combining up to three different materials in any one project.

Everybody likes to change their surroundings from time to time but not everyone can afford to redecorate a whole room with new furniture, carpets and wallpapers. Transforming tired furnishings need not be expensive; by changing your home accessories it is possible to breathe new life into a room and change the mood and feel of the space around you.

With this in mind Museum Quilts commissioned artist Anny Evason to design a unique range of home furnishing accessories to appeal to a wide variety of tastes and ages. At the same time the designs had to acknowledge the phenomenal popularity of the "country look", and be suitable for a city, suburban or rural country home. As you leaf through the pages of this book you will see that we have peppered the chapters with Anny's original artworks. Remaining as true to the original designs as was practically possible, the authors have carefully turned the designs into reality only making essential changes for ease of sewing.

Using vibrant colors and a unique set of motifs for each chapter, *Cozy Country* offers an imaginative range of functional and decorative furnishing accessories to brighten your home.

The
KITCHEN

A bright color scheme of cobalt blue, rich chrome yellow and creamy white makes for a sun-filled kitchen. These warm mid-summer colors will transform the gloom of a gray winter day and brighten rooms that have poor natural lighting. Offset against a variety of cozy work-a-day flannel plaids I have brought the countryside into the kitchen with well-loved farmyard motifs – ducks, geese and hens. Pride of place in the kitchen sits the Contented Cat's Basket. I've chosen a bright primrose yellow for the walls to add warmth to the stone floor.

GOOSE AND SUNFLOWER TABLECOVER

SIZE 68½ in / 174 cm square

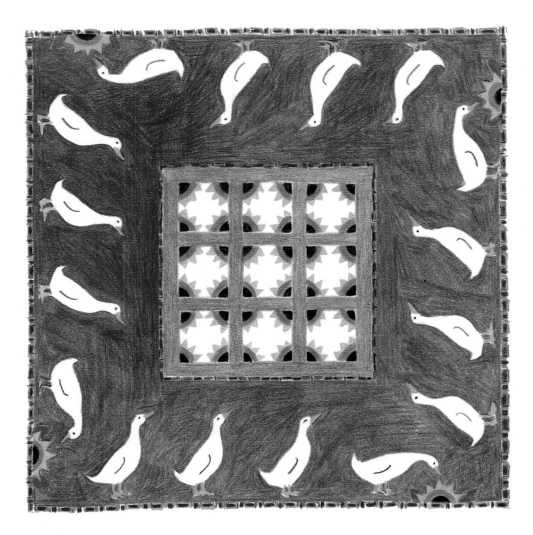

MATERIALS

■ All measurements are based on a fabric width of 45 in / 114.3 cm.

2 yd / 2 m royal blue fine corduroy for the background

1¼ yd / 1.15 m soft white moleskin for the geese

½ yd / 0.5 m bright blue felt for the inner center square

⅔ yd / 0.6 m cotton plaid for binding and the border of the center square

12 × 24 in / 30 × 60 cm yellow washable felt for the center panel

12 × 24 in / 30 × 60 cm orange washable felt

8 × 12 in / 20 × 30 cm brown washable felt

5 × 7 in / 12 × 18 cm green washable felt

3 yd / 3 m fusible webbing

Cardboard to make templates

CUTTING

■ Before cutting, dampen all wool and corduroy fabrics and iron dry to prevent shrinkage when washing. Read the General Techniques chapter for instructions on making templates, using fusible webbing, and appliqué.

1. Make templates for each motif.

2. From the royal blue corduroy, cut four lengths 18½ × 70 in / 47 × 178 cm.

3. From the white fabric cut nine 7 in / 17.8 cm squares.

4. Bond fusible webbing to the reverse of the remaining white fabric. Place the geese templates right side down on the wrong side of the fabric and mark an outline. Cut twelve upright geese and four pecking geese.

5. From the bright blue, cut six strips 2¼ × 7 in / 5.7 × 17.8 cm. Cut four strips 2¼ × 23½ in / 5.7 × 59.1 cm, and two strips 2¼ × 27 in / 5.7 × 68.6 cm.

6. From the plaid flannel, for the border around the center panel, cut two strips 1½ × 27 in / 3.8 × 68.6 cm, and two strips 1½ × 29 in / 3.8 × 73.7 cm. For the binding cut seven strips 2 × 42 in / 5.1 × 106.7 cm.

7. From yellow felt, using the template provided bond and cut the required number of feet and bills for the geese. Bond and cut four large flower petals for the motif at the edge of the tablecover, and 36 corner petals.

8. From the orange felt, use the template provided and bond and cut four large arcs and 36 corner arcs.

9. From the brown felt bond and cut four large semi-circular centers and 36 small quarter-circles.

10. From the green, bond and cut eight leaves.

11. From cardboard, cut one 6½ in / 16.5 cm square to use as a template for the pieced center.

MAKING UP

■ Use a ¼ in / 0.6 cm seam allowance throughout. Pin and baste each step before stitching. Trim and tidy the seam allowances as you work. Press all seams towards the darkest color.

1. To make the center panel, center the cardboard on one white 7 in / 17.8 cm square. Using a light pencil, mark an outline on the felt as a guide to placing the appliqués.

2. Remove the paper backing from the sunflower shapes. Using the pencil line as a guide, position a brown felt quarter-circle in one corner of the square. Add the orange felt corner arc, then the yellow felt petals to make up the flower. Overlap the raw edges by ⅛ in / 0.3 cm and fuse to the background fabric. Satin stitch around each raw edge.

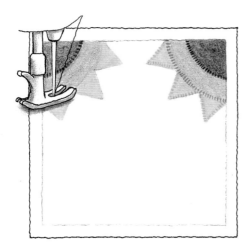

3. Complete one corner at a time, then repeat on each corner of the nine white squares.

4. Stitch a 7 in / 17.8 cm length of bright blue to the bottom of six blocks only. Then make up three vertical rows. Between two rows stitch a 23¼ in / 59.1 cm length. Stitch the third row of blocks to the first two. Stitch each remaining 23¼ in / 59.1 cm length to the top and bottom of the pieced square. Stitch the 27 in / 68.6 cm lengths to each side.

cover. Tuck the feet and bills under the body of each goose. Position the flowers ¾ in / 1.9 cm away from the raw edge as before. Bond each motif using a hot iron.

5. To add the plaid border, stitch each 27 in / 68.6 cm length to the top and bottom of the panel. Stitch each 29 in / 73.7 cm length to each side.

6. To position the goose border, place the pieced center right side up on a clean, flat surface. Place the four lengths of corduroy around the pieced center square. Ensure that the nap of the corduroy runs in the same direction throughout.

7. Mark the center of each side of the pieced top and center of each corduroy length with pins. Fold in half and press very lightly. Match the center points.

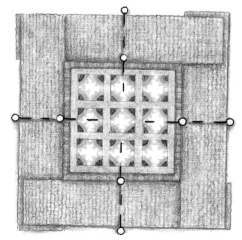

8. With right sides together stitch one length to one side of the pieced border starting and ending ¼ in / 0.6 cm from the top and bottom of the center square. Stitch each of the three remaining borders to the center panel in the same way, taking care not to catch in the excess fabric at each corner. Press the entire piece.

9. To miter the corners, follow the instructions on page 110. On the wrong side of the tablecover trim the excess fabric from the seam allowance.

10. Position the appliqué motifs. Each goose body should be 2 in / 5.1 cm away from the outside raw edge of the

11. Use a narrow satin stitch and complementary color to machine appliqué around each raw edge. Satin stitch the eyes on each goose.

12. To make continuous binding, follow the instructions on page 108.

13. With right sides and raw edges together, and the fold of the binding facing the pieced center, and starting 6 in / 15.2 cm from the bottom left-hand side, stitch the binding to the front of the tablecover. Follow the instructions on page 110 in the General Techniques chapter to miter each of the four corners.

14. Fold the binding over the stitching line to the back of the tablecover and slipstitch in place, mitering each corner as you work.

THE CAT'S BASKET

MATERIALS

■ Before buying fabric read and
understand the instructions for
measuring your basket in steps 1–2
to determine the required yardage of
all materials.

Plaid flannel for basket liner

Blue corduroy for the cushion and
binding

Russet and fawn corduroy scraps for
the mice decoration

Flannel or light-weight cotton for
backing

Elastic ¼ in / 0.6 cm wide

Thin, low loft batting

Scraps of fusible webbing

Black beads for eyes

One bag of cushion stuffing

Double-sided tape

DETERMINING YARDAGE

1. Measure the length and width of the bottom of the basket and add to your measurement 1 in / 2.5 cm. For an oval or round shape you may find it easier to make a template of the inside bottom of the basket.

2. Measure the circumference of the inside top of your basket and add to this 1 in / 2.5 cm. To determine the depth of the lining, place the tape measure under the lip on the outside of the basket and carry the tape over the lip and down the inner side of the basket. To this measurement add a further 1 in / 2.5 cm.

CUTTING

■ Read the General Techniques chapter for instructions on making templates, using fusible webbing, appliqué, and double-fold binding.

1. Make templates from the mice patterns provided.

2. For lining the sides of the basket, cut one piece of plaid the length of your measurement. The width of the plaid should be the same as your measurement from the outside lip to the base of the inner basket. Cut the same from backing and from batting.

3. From the same plaid fabric, for the bottom of the basket, cut one piece slightly larger than your template. Cut the same from the backing and from the batting.

4. From the blue corduroy, to make the cushion, use your template for the bottom of the basket and cut two shapes. Measure around the circumference of the basket bottom and add to this measurement 1 in / 2.5 cm. Cut one strip the length of your measurement × 2¼ in / 5.7 cm wide for the cushion side.

5. From the blue corduroy, for binding the outer edge of the plaid liner, cut one strip 1 in / 2.5 cm longer than the length of the plaid fabric × 1½ in / 3.8 cm wide. For ties, cut four strips 1 × 7 in / 2.5 × 17.8 cm.

6. If your basket has an opening to one side, measure the sides and bottom of the opening and add 1 in / 2.5 cm to your measurement. Cut a length of blue corduroy 2 in / 5.1 cm wide × the length of your measurement to bind the opening.

7. Bond the fusible webbing to the reverse of the russet and fawn corduroy and cut the required number of mice and ears.

MAKING UP

■ Use a ½ in / 1.3 cm seam allowance throughout unless otherwise stated. Pin and baste each step before stitching. Stitch fabrics together with right sides facing.

1. Before adding the mice and ears to the plaid liner, fold the liner in half widthways, then in half again and mark the center and quarter points. Fuse the small mice to the plaid. Satin stitch around the raw edges and define the legs and top of the head. Add the contrasting ear and appliqué around the edge. Stitch on the eyes.

2. To make up the liner for the sides and for the bottom of the basket, sandwich the plaid, batting and backing together. Baste securely. Without stitching over the mice on the side liner, machine quilt the layers 1 in / 2.5 cm apart and following the lines of the plaid. Try the liner for size in the basket and adjust the seam accordingly. Stitch the two short ends of the side liner together and match the lines of the plaid to ensure a neat and accurate finish.

3. If your basket has slanting sides, fit the liner by pleating and pinning the bottom.

4. If your basket has a front opening, align the seam with the center of the opening and allowing ½ in / 1.3 cm seam at each edge, cut away the fabric from the basket opening.

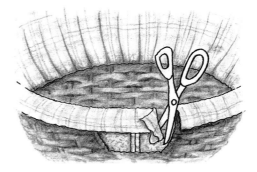

5. To bind the opening, stitch a guideline ½ in / 1.3 cm from the raw edge. Reinforce the corner stitching. Clip the corners at a diagonal in the seam allowance. Do not breach the stitched guideline.

6. To prepare the binding for the opening, fold the strip of blue corduroy in half lengthways and press. Turn in the raw edges to the pressed center line and press again.

15

7. To bind the opening, start at the top left-hand side and with right sides together pin the raw edge of the binding to the raw edge of the plaid as far as the first corner. The clipped corners will allow you to open the three sides of the opening out to a straight line. Pin the binding across the entire opening. Stitch the binding to the plaid on the first foldline.

allowances, and for an neat appearance, machine overcast the raw edge to finish.

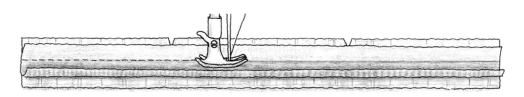

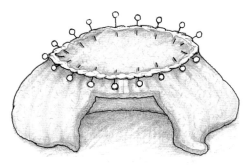

8. Trim the raw edges of the plaid to ¼ in / 0.6 cm. Fold the binding over to the back of the liner and hand stitch in place covering the first stitching line. To miter the corners, coax the excess binding into a corner fold – use a fine knitting needle. Secure with a few hand stitches.

10. Open out the folded edge and align the raw edge with that of the plaid. Pin. Trim the binding to the required length. Turn under ¼ in / 0.6 cm at the other short end and machine stitch. Fold the binding over the stitching line to the back of the liner. Pin. Machine topstitch.

13. Fit the liner to the basket and pull the elastic until the liner fits snugly under the lip at the outside of the basket. Stitch the elastic in place.

14. To make the ties, turn under a ¼ in / 0.6 cm seam to the wrong side of the blue corduroy and machine stitch to hold. Stitch each tie to the top of the front opening. Thread through the basket and tie at the front.

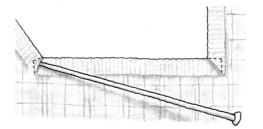

MAKING THE CUSHION

9. Stitch a guideline around the top of the plaid liner ¼ in / 0.6 cm from the raw edge. For binding and casing turn under ¼ in / 0.6 cm on one short edge of royal blue corduroy and stitch to hold. Turn under and press ¼ in / 0.6 cm on one long edge, and overcast the other edge by machine.

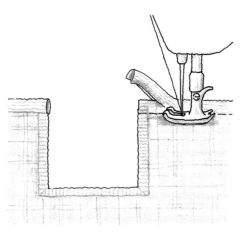

1. Fold the cushion pieces in half and half again. Mark the center points.

2. Stitch together the two short edges of the cushion side using the strip cut in step 4 of Cutting. With right sides facing, pin then stitch the binding to the cushion front. Stitch on the other half of the cushion. Leave a gap to turn and stuff.

11. Thread elastic through the casing. Stitch to hold in place at one end, ½ in / 1.3 cm from the starting point. Leave the elastic loose at the other end until the final fitting.

3. Clip into the seam allowance to help the seam lie flat. Turn the cushion right side out and fill with polyester cushion filling. Slipstitch across the opening.

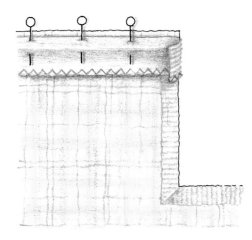

12. To complete the basket liner, match and mark the center and side points of the lining with those on the liner bottom. Pin the side piece and the bottom together as illustrated, and check the fit in your basket. Adjust the seams where necessary. Baste the two pieces together, and then machine stitch using ¼ in / 0.6 cm seam allowance. Trim any bulky seam

4. To finish, using any remaining scrap fabric fuse a backing to the large mouse, trim and stick to the side of the basket with double-sided tape.

PIECED SUNFLOWER RUG

SIZE 31 × 44½ in / 78.7 × 113 cm

MATERIALS

■ All measurements are based on a fabric width of 45 in / 114.3 cm.

1¼ yd / 1.15 m navy corduroy for the background

⅔ yd / 0.6 m royal blue corduroy

Two 18 in / 46 cm squares of gold washable felt for the motifs

One 18 in / 46 cm square of dark brown washable felt

12 × 24 in / 30 × 60 cm of light golden brown corduroy

½ yd / 0.5 m emerald green for binding and appliqué motifs

Scrap of red felt (2¼ × 1½ in / 5.7 × 3.8 cm) for one triangle

32 × 46 in / 81 × 113 cm backing fabric

32 × 46 in / 81 × 113 cm pelmet-weight Vilene

Two pieces batting 32 × 46 in / 81 × 113 cm – an old blanket will do

9 yd / 8.25 m of fusible webbing

CUTTING

■ Before cutting, dampen all wool and corduroy fabrics and iron dry to prevent shrinkage when washing. Read the General Techniques chapter for instructions on making templates, using fusible webbing and appliqué. Bond fusible webbing to the reverse of each fabric shape as you work, then cut the excess webbing away.

1. Make templates for all the appliqué shapes. Place the templates right side down on the wrong side of the fabric and mark an outline. Cut the required number of each from fabric. Repeat, cutting slightly larger templates from fusible webbing.

2. Bond fusible webbing to the wrong side of the rug top. Cut the navy corduroy 32 × 45 in / 81.3 × 114.3 cm.

3. From the royal blue corduroy and from fusible webbing, cut six 10½ in / 26.7 cm squares. Bond the fusible webbing to the wrong side, then cut the squares to 10 in / 25.4 cm exactly.

4. Bond the gold felt and cut 20 continuous triangular strips. Bond and cut four green triangular strips, five single triangles in royal blue and one red triangle.

5. Bond and cut 24 gold sawtooth petals, 24 dark brown corner flower centers, and 24 golden brown corduroy corner flower arcs.

MAKING UP

1. To make the motifs on the royal blue squares, bond all the sunflower motifs one corner at a time.

18

2. Remove the backing from the fusible web. Pin all the pieces of the flower motifs in place, ensuring that the petals overlap by ⅛ in / 0.3 cm. Bond in place and appliqué over the joins and each inner raw edge using narrow satin stitch.

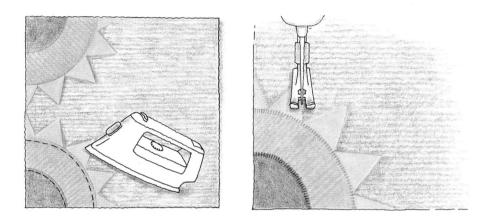

3. To place the sunflower blocks on the foundation fabric, spread the navy blue corduroy fabric out on a clean, flat surface. Measure and mark with basting stitches 4 in / 10.2 cm from each raw edge. Place one square in each corner, joining up to the basting line. Center the two remaining squares between the corner blocks. Pin all the squares in place. Do not bond at this stage.

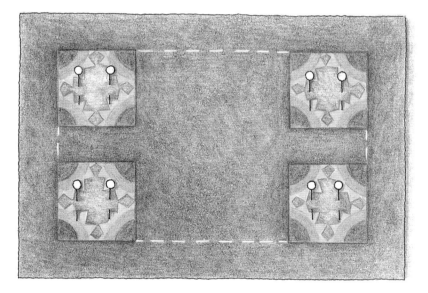

4. Position each sawtooth border around the raw edge of each square, ensuring that the square overlaps the edge of the border by ⅛ in / 0.3 cm. Use the color photograph as a guide to position each color. Where the sawtooth edging is multi-colored, cut away single triangles from the continuous length and replace these with individual triangles. Appliqué over the raw edges and over the joins.

5. To layer the rug, bond fusible webbing to the wrong side of the backing, and bond to one piece of batting. Bond the rug front to the second piece of batting. Between the layers place the pelmet-weight Vilene. For instructions on making continuous binding, binding the rug sandwich and making mitered corners see pages 108 and 110. Make up 4½ yd / 4.1 m of binding 2½ in / 6.4 cm wide.

NESTING HEN CUSHION

SIZE 16½ × 16½ in / 41.9 × 41.9 cm

MATERIALS

■ All measurements are based on a fabric width of 45 in / 114.3 cm.

⅔ yd / 0.6 m light blue corduroy for the cushion top and back

3 × 10 in / 8 × 25 cm turquoise cotton for the appliqué motifs

12 in / 30 cm square white washable felt

6 × 11 in / 15 × 28 cm gold felt

4 × 5 in / 9 × 13 cm orange felt

7 × 12 in / 17 × 30 cm royal blue corduroy

5 × 13 in / 13 × 33 cm brighter-than-navy corduroy

4 × 11 in / 10 × 28 cm chestnut brown felt

3 × 8 in / 8 × 20 cm colonial blue felt

Small scrap cherry red

1 yd / 1 m fusible webbing

Three blue buttons ½ in / 1.3 cm diameter for fastening

Embroidery floss

CUTTING

■ Before cutting, dampen all fabrics and iron dry to prevent shrinkage. Read the General Techniques chapter for instructions on making and using templates, working with fusible webbing, and appliqué.

1. From the light blue, for the front and back, cut two 17½ in / 44.5 cm squares. For the flap, cut one rectangle 6½ × 17½ in / 16.5 × 44.5 cm.

2. From the brighter-than navy, for the left-hand border cut one strip 2⅛ × 11¾ in / 5.4 × 29.9 cm, and for the right-hand border, cut one strip 2⅛ × 12¼ in / 5.4 × 31.1 cm.

3. From the royal blue, for the top and bottom borders cut two strips 2⅛ × 12 in / 5.4 × 30.5 cm. Cut one corner motif (Template F) from fabric and fusible webbing. Fuse together.

4. Iron fusible webbing to the reverse of each remaining fabric. Do not remove the paper backing at this stage. From the turquoise, cut 17 squares each 1 in / 2.5 cm.

5. From the white, cut one chicken and one wing. We used pinking shears to cut out the wing. Cut 17 squares 1 × 1 in / 2.5 × 2.5 cm.

6. From the gold, cut the straw nest (Template D). Cut one square 1 in / 2.5 cm, and cut two corner motifs (Templates E and H).

7. From the orange felt, cut one wattle and one comb. Cut one corner motif (Template G).

8. From the chestnut brown, cut one basket (Template C). Cut one square 2½ in / 6.4 cm for the bottom right-hand corner.

9. From the colonial blue, cut one square 2⅜ in / 6.7 cm for the top left-hand corner. Cut one rectangle 2½ × 2¼ in / 6.4 × 5.7 cm for the top right-hand corner. Cut one rectangle 2¼ × 2⅜ in / 5.7 × 6 cm for the bottom left-hand corner.

10. From the cherry red, cut one square 1 in / 2.5 cm.

MAKING UP

1. To prepare the top border strip, stitch a guideline ¼ in / 0.6 cm from one long edge and one short edge.

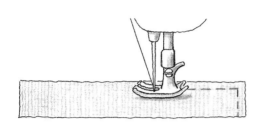

2. Arrange one gold square and eight turquoise squares on one strip of royal blue. The squares should be turned on-point and should join up to the stitched guidelines and to each other.

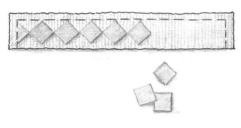

3. Remove the paper backing from each and bond in position. Using a narrow satin stitch, appliqué over the raw edges of each square.

4. Repeat steps 1–3, fusing nine turquoise squares to the remaining royal blue strip for the bottom border. In the same way for the left-hand border fuse eight white squares and one cherry red square to the brighter-than-navy. For the right-hand border, fuse nine white squares to the remaining border strip.

5. To make the corners, fuse the orange motif to the colonial blue square, the gold motifs to the colonial blue rectangles and the royal blue motif to the dark brown square. Machine appliqué around each.

6. To attach the appliqué borders and corners to the cushion, first stitch a

line 1⅝ in / 4.1 cm from the outside raw edges of the cushion front. This is your placement line.

7. With right sides facing, pin each border strip to the cushion front so that the stitched guidelines are aligned with each other.

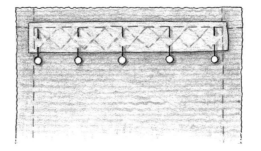

8. Sew over each stitched guideline reinforcing the edges with extra stitching, then press back each border.

9. Position each corner so that it covers the raw edges of the border strips. They should be inset ½ in / 1.3 cm from the raw edges of the cushion.

10. To make up the chicken, bond the wing to the body and satin stitch from dot to dot.

11. Position the basket, straw nest, chicken and comb in the center of the cushion front so that each piece is just tucked under the shape it joins on to. Fuse in place. Position the wattle, fuse and satin stitch around the edges.

12. To make the eye, using four strands of embroidery floss stem stitch a small circle. To finish, using royal blue thread, stitch small stab stitches around the outline of the chicken. (See Stitch Glossary.)

13. To make up the cushion, follow the instructions in the General Techniques section on page 110. Use a ½ in / 1.3 cm seam allowance.

SITTING HEN TEA COZY

SIZE 10½ × 13 in / 26.7 × 33 cm excluding the hen

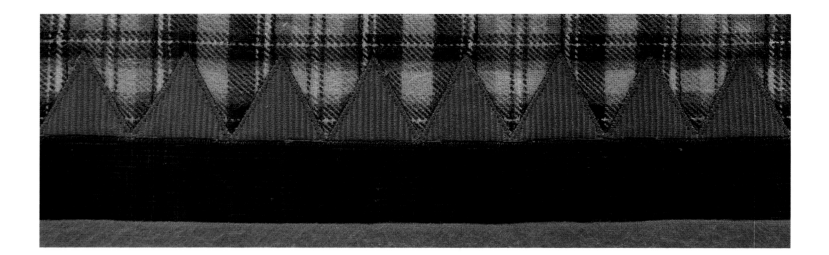

MATERIALS

■ All measurements are based on a fabric width of 45 in / 114.3 cm.

½ yd / 0.5 m plaid flannel for the tea cozy

⅔ yd / 0.6 m white flannel for the inside lining

15 × 30 in / 38 × 76 cm of 2 oz / 50 gm batting

⅓ yd / 0.3 m pelmet-weight Vilene

⅓ yd / 0.3 m heavy-weight iron-on interfacing

1 yd / 1 m fusible webbing

Scraps of navy and royal blue corduroy for the base

11 × 13 in / 28 × 33 cm gold felt for the hen

10 × 9 in / 25 × 22 cm white felt

Scraps of red and yellow felt for the comb and wattle

2 × 28 in / 5 × 71 cm red flannel to bind the base

Black embroidery floss

Fabric glue

CUTTING

■ Before cutting, dampen all wool and corduroy fabrics and iron dry to prevent shrinkage when washing. Read the General Techniques chapter for instructions on making templates, using fusible webbing, and appliqué.

1. For the tea cozy, place Template A right side down on the right side of the fabric and cut four shapes from the plaid flannel. Cut the same from the white cotton flannel on the lengthways grain. Cut two shapes from interfacing and two slightly larger ones from fusible webbing.

2. From the royal blue corduroy, cut two strips 1 × 14 in / 2.5 × 35.6 cm. From the navy corduroy, cut two strips 1¼ × 14 in / 3.1 × 35.6 cm. Rough cut the same from fusible webbing.

3. To make the hen, place the templates right side down on the right side of the gold and cut each shape. Flip the template over and cut the reverse shape. Repeat, cutting each shape slightly larger from fusible webbing. Cut each shape from Vilene slightly smaller than the template.

MAKING UP

■ Use a ¼ in / 0.6 cm seam allowance throughout. Pin and baste each step before stitching. Trim and tidy the seam allowances as you work. Press all seams towards the darkest color after each step.

1. To make the cozy, fuse the iron-on interfacing to the wrong side of two plaid shapes.

2. Bond fusible webbing to the reverse of the royal blue and the navy strip. Use Template B to cut the sawtooth border from the royal blue. Position the sawtooth strip 1¼ in /

3.2 cm from the bottom raw edge of the tea cozy shape on the right side and fuse together. Place the navy strip below the sawtooth border, so that one overlaps the other by ⅛ in / 0.3 cm and bond together. Appliqué around the raw edges of the border strips. Put to one side.

3. Place one white flannel cozy shape right side down. On top center a piece of batting and the plaid shape with the border right side up on top. Baste the layers together ½ in / 1.3 cm away from the edges. Baste vertical grids of stitches 1½ in / 3.8 cm apart. Repeat for the other side of the cozy.

4. On each side of the cozy, machine quilt channels of vertical stitching down as far as the sawtooth border. Pull the quilting threads to the wrong side and tie in the ends. Remove the basting stitches.

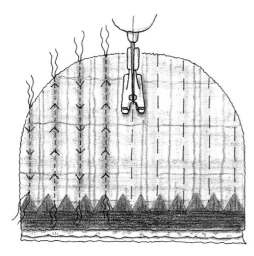

5. With right sides together, baste the quilted cozy shapes together. Stitch around the curved edge, leaving open the bottom edge. Using pinking shears, trim one raw edge to ½ in / 1.3 cm, and the other to ¼ in / 0.6 cm to help reduce bulk. Press the seam allowance open. Turn right side out.

6. To make the lining, bond two fusible webbing shapes to the wrong

side of two plaid shapes. Trim the paper to the exact size of the shape. Remove the paper backing and fuse the two white cotton shapes to each plaid shape. With plaid sides facing, stitch the two pieces together around the curved edge, leaving the straight bottom raw edge open. Turn right side out. Put to one side.

7. Insert the lining into the cozy and baste the bottom raw edges together.

8. To prepare the binding, turn under ¼ in / 0.6 cm seam on one long raw edge and press.

9. Align the remaining raw edge of the binding with the raw edge of the bottom of the cozy, so that right sides are facing. Stitch a seam ¼ in / 0.6 cm from the raw edge. Press. Turn back the binding over the stitching line, over the raw edges to the inside of the cozy. Slipstitch the folded edge in place, so that it covers the line of machine stitching.

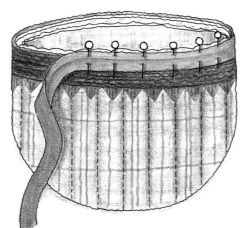

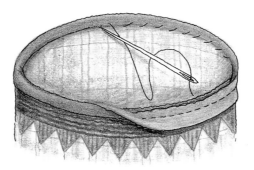

10. To make the hen, bond the Vilene to the wrong side of the felt shapes.

11. Work narrow satin stitch ⅛ in / 0.3 cm from the edge of the nest outline. Work a row of machine straight stitch ½ in / 1.3 cm inside the satin stitch.

12. Using the template as a guide embroider the eye on the hen. Use chain stitch for the outer circle and a French knot for the center. (See Stitch Glossary on page 112.)

13. Position each side of the nest so that it overlaps the base of each hen body by ⅛ in / 0.3 cm. Work satin stitch over the join. Place the red wattle under the neck securing it with fabric glue, then place the comb just under the top of the head. Position the beak. Machine satin stitch over all of the joins.

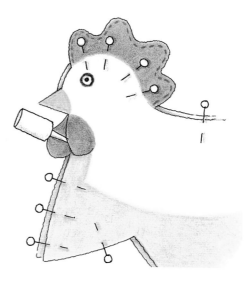

14. With right sides together, stitch the two sides of the sitting hen together between the points marked on the nest template. Leave the bottom of the nest open to fit over the top of the tea cozy.

15. Position the hen over the top of the cozy and anchor the two together with a few holding stitches.

BEE AND SUNFLOWER OVEN MITTS

SIZE 7¾ × 35 in / 19.7 × 88.9 cm

MATERIALS

½ yd / 0.5 m small to medium plaid

½ yd / 0.5 m royal blue corduroy

¾ yd / 0.7 m white flannel for lining

½ yd / 0.5 m 2 oz / 50 gm batting

5 × 7 in / 13 × 18 cm yellow felt for the appliqué motifs

5 × 6 in / 13 × 15 cm orange felt for the appliqué motifs

Fabric scraps for the remaining appliqué motifs

12 in / 30 cm square fusible webbing

One curtain ring for hanging

CUTTING

■ Read the General Techniques chapter carefully for instructions on making and using templates, working with fusible webbing and methods of appliqué.

1. Use the patterns provided to make templates for the appliqué motifs and the oven mitts. Bond and cut the required number of bees and flowers, but do not remove the paper backing at this stage.

2. From the plaid, cut one length 8¼ × 36 in / 21 × 91.4 cm, and four rectangles 8¼ × 9 in / 21 × 22.9 cm. Use the mitt template to shape each end of the 36 in / 91.4 cm length, and one end of each of the four rectangles.

3. From white flannel, cut four rectangles 8¼ × 8¾ in / 21 × 22.2 cm, and two lengths 8¼ × 36 in / 21 × 91.4 cm.

4. From the royal blue corduroy, cut one length 8¼ × 36 in / 21 × 91.4 cm.

Use the template to shape each end. Cut the same from batting. For binding, on the cross grain cut two strips 2×40 in / 5.1×101.6 cm, and two strips $2 \times 8\frac{3}{4}$ in / 5.1×22.2 cm.

MAKING UP

■ Use a $\frac{1}{4}$ in / 0.6 cm seam allowance throughout. Pin and baste each step before stitching. Trim and tidy the seam allowances as you work. Press all seams towards the darkest color.

1. Place the 36 in / 91.4 cm length of blue corduroy right side down on a clean, flat surface. On top, aligning all raw edges, place one white flannel length, then the batting, another length of flannel, then two short white flannel lengths at each end, and finally the plaid fabric right side up. These six layers will ensure adequate protection when picking up hot pots and pans. The flannel can be substituted with cuttings from an old woolen blanket or specialist heat-resistant fabrics.

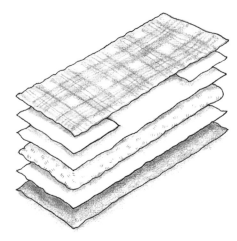

2. Baste all the layers together horizontally, vertically and around all of the edges.

3. Machine quilt the layers evenly with a 1 in / 2.5 cm horizontal and vertical grid.

4. Trim the mitt to measure $7\frac{3}{4} \times 35$ in / 19.7×88.9 cm.

5. Before making up the hand pocket shapes, bond and appliqué with narrow satin stitch the motifs to the plaid fabric. To make the bees, bond the black stripes to the body first, then bond to the pocket. Satin stitch the antennae.

6. Layer and baste the fabrics together for each pocket shape; plaid, batting, flannel, and the appliquéd top. Machine quilt a 1 in / 2.5 cm grid on each pocket shape using the lines of the plaid as your guide and avoiding the appliqué motifs. Hand quilt $\frac{1}{8}$ in / 0.3 cm around the edge of each sunflower and bee motif. Pull the ends

of the quilting thread through to the back of the work and tie off the loose ends. Trim each pocket to measure $7\frac{3}{4} \times 8\frac{3}{4}$ in / 19.7×22.2 cm.

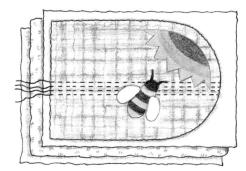

7. Read the instructions in the General Techniques chapter on double-fold binding on page 109, and bind the pocket on the short straight edge only. Machine topstitch $\frac{1}{2}$ in / 1.3 cm from the outer edge.

8. To make the binding for the whole oven mitt, stitch the two 40 in / 101.6 cm lengths of corduroy together with a diagonal seam.

9. Pin and baste each pocket to each end of the mitt. Stitch the pockets to the mitt using a $\frac{3}{8}$ in / 1 cm seam. Secure with a second row $\frac{1}{8}$ in / 0.3 cm from the raw edge.

10. Prepare the binding following the instructions in the General Techniques chapter on page 109. When binding curved edges, ease the binding around the curve. Overlap the start and end of the binding by $\frac{1}{2}$ in / 1.3 cm.

11. Hand stitch the curtain ring to the binding at the center of the mitt.

The LIVING ROOM

A soft, warm and sumptuous elegance is achieved in this living room using a rich and dramatic palette of hot purple shades with tones of fall. Nut brown, russet, cherry red and maroon blend harmoniously with deep plum, purple and bright, vibrant orange. Hot exotic shades in soft flannels, wools and practical, washable felts add a striking glow to our living room decor. Country folk motifs on the cushions and floor rug blend well with the geometric design of the wallhanging.

STRIPED THROW OR WALLHANGING

SIZE 52½ × 53½ in / 132.7 × 135.9 cm

MATERIALS

■ Quantities for wool fabrics are based on a fabric width of 54 in / 137 cm.

¼ yd / 0.25 m maroon red wool A

⅔ yd / 0.6 m wine red wool B

½ yd / 0.5 m soft red cotton moleskin C

¼ yd / 0.25 m cherry red wool D

¼ yd / 0.25 m bright red wool E

4 in / 10 cm orange wool F

½ yd / 0.5 m fawn corduroy G

6 × 18 in / 15 × 20 cm russet corduroy H

5 in / 12 cm square warm brown wool I

½ yd / 0.5 m dark brown wool J

⅔ yd / 0.6 m gunmetal brown wool K

½ yd / 0.5 m dark brown corduroy L

⅔ yd / 0.6 m purple washable felt M

4 in / 10 cm lavender wool N

7 in / 18 cm square shocking pink O

10 × 6 in / 25 × 15 cm deep purple wool P

2 yd / 2 m fusible webbing

½ yd / 0.5 m brown for binding

1½ yd / 1.4 m of 54 in / 137 cm wide strong cotton for backing

■ The throw is made up of 13 sections which are pieced together into seven panels. Use the black and white line illustration as a guide.

CUTTING

■ Wash all fabrics separately first. Read the General Techniques chapter on making templates, using fusible webbing and appliqué. Label each piece with each measurement and section as you cut, and keep each section separate. Cut the largest measurements from your fabric first.

1. From maroon red wool A, for section 4, bond and cut one triangular strip using Template 4(a). Cut one strip 2½ × 7¾ in / 6.4 × 19.7 cm.
For section 5, cut one strip 2½ × 16 in / 6.4 × 40.6 cm.
For section 12, cut six rectangles 3¼ × 4 in / 8.3 × 10.2 cm.

2. From wine red wool B, for section 1, cut two strips 3 × 1½ in / 7.6 × 3.8 cm, two strips 6 × 1½ in / 15 × 3.8 cm, and one square 1½ in / 3.8 cm.
For section 2, cut one strip 1¼ × 22½ in / 3.2 × 57.2 cm. Cut four rectangles 4½ × 4¼ in / 11.4 × 10.8 cm. Bond and cut three strips ¾ × 3¼ in / 2 × 8.3 cm.
For section 3, cut one strip 2 × 8¼ in / 5.1 × 21 cm.
For section 4, cut one strip 1¾ × 7¾ in / 4.4 × 19.7 cm.
For section 5, cut one strip 1¾ × 16 in / 4.4 × 40.6 cm and one strip 3¾ × 16 in / 9.5 × 40.6 cm.
For section 7, cut one strip 1½ × 2 in / 3.8 × 5.1 cm, and one strip 1½ × 2½ in / 3.8 × 6.4 cm.
For section 8, cut nine rectangles 2¾ × 4 in / 7 × 10.2 cm. Cut one strip 2¾ × 54 in / 7 × 137.2 cm.
For section 9, cut one strip 2 × 18½ in / 5.1 × 47 cm.

For section 10, cut one rectangular shape 1¼ × 3 in / 3.1 × 7.6 cm, and one strip 1½ × 13½ in / 3.8 × 34.3 cm.

For section 11, cut one strip 1¼ × 4 in / 3.1 × 10.2 cm.

For section 12, cut five rectangles 4½ × 4 in / 11.4 × 10.2 cm, and one strip 1¼ × 4 in / 3.1 × 10.2 cm.

For section 13, cut one strip 1½ × 3¼ in / 3.8 × 8.3 cm, and one strip 1½ × 4½ in / 3.8 × 11.4 cm.

3. From soft red moleskin C, for section 1, cut one strip 1½ × 6½ in / 3.8 × 16.5 cm.

For section 2, bond and cut one strip 3 × 18 in / 7.6 × 45.7 cm and from this cut eight triangles using Template 2.

For section 3, cut one strip 3 × 8¼ in / 7.6 × 21 cm.

For section 4, cut one strip 3 × 7¾ in / 7.6 × 19.7 cm, and one square 3 × 3 in / 7.6 × 7.6 cm.

For section 5, bond and cut one strip 13 × 3½ in / 33 × 8.9 cm and from this use Template 5 and cut a continuous length of four triangles. Bond and cut one single triangle. Cut one strip 3½ × 16 in / 8.9 × 40.6 cm.

For section 8, bond and cut one strip 3½ × 20 in / 8.9 × 50.5 cm from this cut ten triangles using Template 8.

For section 11, cut one strip 3 × 18½ in / 7.6 × 47 cm.

For section 12, bond and cut one strip 3½ × 12 in / 8.9 × 30.5 cm and from this cut five triangular shapes using Template 12.

4. From cherry red wool D, for section 1, cut one strip 1½ × 3¾ in / 3.8 × 9.5 cm and one strip 1½ × 3½ in / 3.8 × 8.9 cm.

For section 2, cut three rectangles 3½ × 3¼ in / 8.9 × 8.3 cm. Cut one strip 1¼ × 22½ in / 3.1 × 57.2 cm.

For section 13, cut one strip 3¾ × 1½ in / 9.5 × 3.8 cm, and one strip 2 × 1½ in / 5.1 × 3.8 cm.

5. From bright red wool E, for section 1, cut one strip 1½ × 5 in / 3.8 × 12.7 cm, and one strip 1½ × 1¼ in / 3.8 × 3.1 cm. Cut one rectangle 4½ × 5½ in / 11.4 × 14 cm.

For section 5, cut one strip 1¼ × 16 in / 3.8 × 40.6 cm.

For section 7, cut one square 1½ in / 3.8 cm, and one strip 1½ × 2 in / 3.8 × 5.1 cm.

For section 10, cut one strip 1½ × 2½ in / 3.8 × 6.4 cm.

For section 13, cut one strip 1½ × 3½ in / 3.8 × 8.9 cm, one strip 5¾ × 1½ in / 14.6 × 3.8 cm, and one strip 4¾ × 1½ in / 12.1 × 3.8 cm. Cut one rectangular shape 4½ × 6½ in / 11.4 × 16.5 cm.

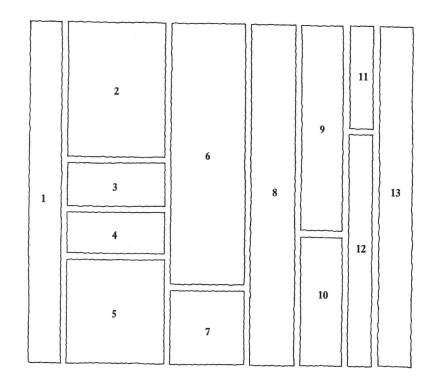

Use this illustration as a guide to stitching the sections together.

6. From orange wool F, for section 2, use Template 2 and bond and cut five triangles.

For section 8, bond and cut nine small triangles using Template 8.

For section 10, cut one rectangle 1½ × 1¾ in / 3.8 × 4.4 cm.

For section 12, bond and cut six small triangles using Template 12.

7. From fawn corduroy G, for section 2, cut one strip 1½ × 23½ in / 3.8 × 56.7 cm.

For section 3, bond and cut one continuous triangular strip using Template 3. Cut one strip 2 × 8¼ in / 5.1 × 21 cm.

For section 4, cut one strip 1 × 7¾ in / 2.5 × 19.7 cm.

For section 5, use Template 5 to bond and cut one continuous triangular strip consisting of five whole and two half triangles.

For section 6, cut one strip 1½ × 33 in / 3.8 × 83.8 cm. Bond and cut the small tree.

For section 7, bond and cut the large tree.

For section 9, cut one strip 1¼ × 16 in / 3.1 × 40.6 cm.

For section 10, cut one square 6¾ × 6¾ in / 17.1 × 17.1 cm.

For section 11, using Template 11 bond and cut one continuous triangular strip consisting of six whole triangles and two half triangles.

8. From russet corduroy H, for section 4, cut one strip 1¼ × 7¾ in / 3.1 × 19.7 cm.

For section 6, cut one strip 2½ × 33 in / 6.4 × 83.8 cm.

For section 9, cut one strip 1½ × 16 in / 3.8 × 40.6 cm.

For section 10, bond and cut one square 3¾ × 3¾ in / 9.5 × 9.5 cm.

For section 13, cut one strip 1½ × 4¼ in / 3.8 × 10.8 cm.

9. From warm brown wool I, for section 3, bond and cut one square 5 × 5 in / 12.7 × 12.7 cm.

10. From dark brown wool J, for section 1, cut two strips 1¼ × 1½ in / 3.1 × 3.8 cm, and one square 1½ × 1½ in / 3.8 × 3.8 cm. Cut one strip 3½ × 1½ in / 8.9 × 3.8 cm, one strip 2 × 1½ in / 5.1 × 3.8 cm, and one strip 2¼ × 1½ in / 5.7 × 3.8 cm.

For section 2, cut one strip 1¼ × 22½ in / 3.1 × 57.2 cm. Cut one strip for the top 7¼ × 1½ in / 18.4 × 3.8 cm.

For section 3, cut one square 8¼ × 8¼ in / 21 × 21 cm.

For section 4, cut one square 7¾ × 7¾ in / 19.7 × 19.7 cm, and one strip 1¼ × 7¾ in / 3.1 × 19.7 cm.

For section 5, cut one strip 1¼ × 16 in / 3.1 × 40.6 cm.

For section 6, cut two strips 2 × 33 in / 5.1 × 83.8 cm.

For section 7, cut one strip 1½ × 3 in / 3.8 × 7.6 cm, and two squares 1½ × 1½ in / 3.8 × 3.8 cm.

For section 8, cut one strip 1¾ × 54 in / 4.4 × 137.2 cm.

For section 9, cut one strip 1¼ × 16 in / 3.1 × 40.6 cm.

For section 10, cut one rectangle 1½ × 1¾ in / 3.8 × 4.4 cm.

For section 13, cut one strip 1½ × 2½ in / 3.8 × 6.4 cm. Cut one strip 1½ × 2¾ in / 3.8 × 7 cm. Cut one strip 1½ × 4½ in / 3.8 × 11.4 cm, and one strip 1½ × 5 in / 3.8 × 12.7 cm.

11. From gunmetal brown wool K, for section 1, cut one strip 4½ × 49 in / 11.4 × 124.5 cm.

For section 6, cut two strips 2 × 33 in / 5.1 × 83.8 cm.

For section 7, cut one piece 11 × 11½ in / 27.9 × 29.2 cm.

For section 13, cut one strip 4½ × 48 in / 11.4 × 121.9 cm.

12. From dark brown corduroy L, for section 1, cut one strip 1½ × 9 in / 3.8 × 22.9 cm.

For section 2, cut one strip 2¼ × 22½ in / 5.7 × 57.2 cm

For section 3, cut one strip 1½ × 8¼ in / 3.8 × 21 cm.

For section 4, bond and cut two triangles using Template 4(b).

For section 5, cut one strip 2¾ × 16 in / 7 × 40.6 cm.

For section 8, cut ten rectangles 3¾ × 4 in / 9.5 × 10.2 cm.

For section 10, cut one strip 2 × 13½ in / 5.1 × 34.3 cm.

For section 11, cut one strip 1½ × 18½ in / 3.8 × 47 cm.

For section 13, cut one strip 1½ × 5¼ in / 3.8 × 13.3 cm.

13. From purple wool M, for section 2, cut three rectangles 3¼ × 3½ in / 8.3 × 8.9 cm. Cut one strip 3 × 22½ in / 7.6 × 57.2 cm.

For section 3, bond and cut one square 3½ × 3½ in / 8.9 × 8.9 cm.

For section 4, bond and cut one square 5 × 5 in / 12.7 × 12.7 cm.

For section 5, cut one strip 2½ × 16 in / 6.4 × 40.6 cm.

For section 6, cut one strip 3 × 33 in / 7.6 × 83.8 cm, and one rectangle 9½ × 10 in / 24.1 × 25.4 cm.

For section 9, cut one strip 4¼ × 34 in / 10.8 × 86.4 cm.

For section 10, cut one strip 4¼ × 13½ in / 10.8 × 34.3 cm.

14. From lavender wool N, for section 6, cut one strip 1½ × 41½ in / 3.8 × 105.4 cm.

For section 9, cut one strip 1½ × 18½ in / 3.8 × 47 cm.

15. From shocking pink O, for section 1, bond and cut one square 2 × 2 in / 5.1 × 5.1 cm.

For section 3, bond and cut one square 2½ × 2½ in / 6.4 × 6.4 cm.

For section 5, using Template 5 bond and cut a single triangle.

For section 13, bond and cut one square 2 × 2 in / 5.1 × 5.1 cm.

16. From purple wool P, for section 2, cut three rectangles 3¼ × 4½ in / 8.3 × 11.4 cm.

For section 3, cut one strip 1½ × 8¼ in / 3.8 × 21 cm.

MAKING UP

■ Use a ¼ in / 0.6 cm seam allowance throughout. Pin and baste each step before stitching. Appliqué around the outline of each shape using narrow satin stitch. Trim and tidy the seam allowances as you work. Press all seams towards the darkest color. Use the line drawing on page 32 as a guide to color placement.

1. To make section 1, bond the 2 in / 5.1 cm square fabric O, to the 4½ × 5½ in / 11.4 × 14 cm rectangle fabric E. Stitch the rectangle to the 49 in / 124.5 cm length of fabric K. Make the pieced outer edge, stitching the 1½ in / 3.8 cm pieces in the order shown. Stitch the two lengths together.

2. To make section 2, stitch each 22½ in / 57.2 cm strip together in the order shown. Stitch the 7¼ × 1½ in / 18.4 × 3.8 cm fabric J to one end. To make the left-hand border, stitch together the rectangles along the 3½ in / 8.9 cm edge. For the right-hand border stitch the 4½ in / 11.4 cm edges together. Bond the triangles and the fabric strips B to the background fabric and appliqué the raw edges. Stitch the borders to the central strip.

3. To make section 3, bond the squares together. Bond and appliqué the triangular strip to its background. Stitch the pieces together as shown along the 8¼ in / 21 cm edge.

4. To make section 4, bond the two triangles to fabric C square. Bond the squares together. Bond the triangular

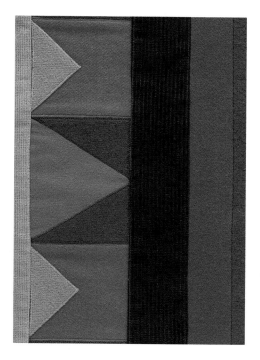

strip to fabric C. Appliqué all the bonded fabrics before stitching the strips and square together.

5. To make section 5, bond and appliqué the continuous triangular strip to the appropriate background fabric. Stitch the strips together.

6. Bond and appliqué the small tree to the large rectangle. Stitch the shorter lengths together. Stitch the rectangle to the pieced strips. Stitch fabric strip N to the right-hand side.

7. For section 7, bond and appliqué the tree to the large rectangle. Stitch the pieced strip together in the order shown and stitch it to the tree rectangle. Sew section 7 to section 6.

8. Stitch the rectangles together on the 4 in / 10.2 cm edge in the order shown. Bond each triangle to the appropriate background fabric. Stitch together the 54 in / 137.2 cm lengths, then stitch the two sections together.

9. To make section 9, stitch fabric B to fabric strip N. Stitch fabric strip H

to fabric J and then to fabric G. Stitch the two strips together at the short end. Stitch the pieced strip to fabric strip M.

10. To make section 10, bond and appliqué the three squares. Stitch the three short strips together at the 1½ in / 3.8 cm edge. Stitch the three 13½ in / 34.3 cm lengths together in the order shown. Stitch the three pieces together.

11. To make section 11, bond and appliqué the continuous triangular strip to fabric strip C, and stitch to strip L. Stitch fabric strip B across the base.

12. To make section 12, stitch the rectangles together in the order shown. Stitch the short fabric strip B to one end. Bond and appliqué the triangles to the appropriate background fabric.

13. To make section 13, stitch the color blocks together in the order shown, along the 1½ in / 3.8 cm edge. Stitch the pieced strip to fabric K. Bond and appliqué the two squares and stitch to the bottom of the pieced strip.

14. Stitch the 13 sections together in the order shown in the line drawing on page 33. Trim loose threads on the wrong side, reduce bulky seams if necessary and press carefully.

15. Make 6 yd / 6 m of 2½ in / 6.4 cm wide continuous single-fold binding.

16. Spread the backing fabric out right side down. Center the pieced panel right side up on top. Baste the two layers together. Bind the throw, following the instructions on pages 109 and 110 of the General Techniques. To make the throw into a wallhanging you will need a hanging sleeve (See page 55).

OLD OAK TREE CUSHION

SIZE 16 × 15 in / 40.6 × 38.1 cm

MATERIALS

- All measurements are based on a fabric width of 45 in / 114.3 cm.

¾ yd / 0.7 m brown wool flannel for the cushion background

¾ yd / 0.7 m fusible webbing

16 in / 40 cm square cushion pad

Three brown buttons ¾ in / 2 cm

18 × 22 in / 46 × 56 cm burnt orange corduroy for the tree

Scraps of different colors for the appliqué borders

17 in / 43 cm square tearaway stabilizer

CUTTING

- Before cutting, dampen all wool and corduroy fabrics and iron dry to prevent shrinkage when washing. Read the General Techniques chapter on pages 105 and 106 for instructions on making templates, using fusible webbing, and appliqué.

1. From the brown wool, cut one piece 17 × 17 in / 43.2 × 43.2 cm for the cushion front. For the back, cut one piece 15½ × 17 in / 39.4 × 43.2 cm, and one piece 7 × 17 in / 17.8 × 43.2 cm.

2. Use the template to cut one tree from fabric and fusible webbing. Bond the webbing to the wrong side of the tree, then cut to the exact size.

3. From fabric scraps cut four squares each 3 × 3 in / 7.6 × 7.6 cm for the corners. Cut each square across the diagonal to make eight triangles. Cut each triangle across the diagonal to make 16 smaller triangles. Cut the acorns from scraps.

4. To make the random borders, cut rectangles of scraps 1½ in / 3.8 cm wide and in varying lengths, sufficient to make four borders measuring 10 × 1½ in / 25.4 × 3.8 cm each.

MAKING UP

- Use a ¼ in / 0.6 cm seam allowance throughout. Pin and baste each step before stitching. Bond all fabrics wrong side to right side. Trim and tidy the seam allowances as you work. Press all seams towards the darkest color after each step.

1. Using any combination of scraps, make up four random borders to measure 10 × 1½ in / 25.4 × 3.8 cm. Iron fusible webbing to the reverse of the borders and trim to the exact size.

2. Bond the four borders and corners to the cushion front, leaving ½ in / 1.3 cm seam allowance all around. Place a sheet of tearaway stabilizer underneath the cushion front to prevent puckers appearing when stitching. Satin stitch the raw edges and the seams.

3. Bond and appliqué the tree and acorns to the center of the cushion. Tear away the stabilizer.

4. To make up the cushion, follow the instructions for the House Cushion on page 40.

HOUSE CUSHION

SIZE   16 × 15 in / 40.6 × 38.1 cm

MATERIALS

■ All measurements are based on a fabric width of 45 in / 114.3 cm.

½ yd / 0.5 m black wool for the cushion background

¾ yd / 0.7 m fusible webbing

16 in / 40 cm square cushion pad

Three black buttons ¾ in / 2 cm

8 × 11 in / 20 × 28 cm peach wool for the borders

7 × 10 in / 18 × 25 cm bright red corduroy for the roof

4 × 9 in / 10 × 22 cm cherry red corduroy for the house side

5 × 8 in / 13 × 20 cm soft red wool for the borders

4 × 8 in / 10 × 20 cm wine red wool for the borders

4 × 8 in / 10 × 20 cm aubergine wool for the borders

6 in / 15 cm square royal blue wool for the borders

8 in / 20 cm square gunmetal brown wool for the borders

5 in / 13 cm square dark brown corduroy for the house

6 × 7 in / 15 × 18 cm russet corduroy for the house

2 in / 5 cm square black corduroy for the house window

CUTTING

■ Before cutting, dampen all wool and corduroy fabrics and iron dry to prevent shrinkage when washing. Read the General Techniques chapter for instructions on using fusible webbing, appliqué, and making templates.

1. Bond fusible webbing to the wrong side of the border and motif fabrics. Do not remove the paper backing. Label each strip as you cut.

2. From the peach, cut five triangles for the left border, six triangles for the right border, and two triangles for the top border. Cut one strip 3 × 2 in / 7.6 × 5.1 cm for the top right corner.

Cut one strip 10½ × 2 in / 26.7 × 5.1 cm for the left border. For the right border, cut one strip 7¼ × 2 in / 18.4 × 5.1 cm, and one strip 2¼ × 2 in / 5.7 × 5.1 cm. Cut two squares 2¼ × 2¼ in / 5.7 × 5.7 cm, one each for the top left and bottom right corners.

10. From the dark brown corduroy, cut two house windows.

11. Cut one house front from the russet corduroy.

12. From the black corduroy, cut one house window.

13. From the black flannel, cut one piece 16 × 17 in / 40.6 × 43.2 cm for the cushion front. For the back, cut one piece 5 × 17 in / 12.7 × 43.2 cm for the flap opening, and one piece 16½ × 17 in / 41.9 × 43.2 cm.

MAKING UP

■ Use a ¼ in / 0.6 cm seam allowance throughout. Pin and baste each step before stitching. Bond all fabrics wrong side to right side. Trim and tidy the seam allowances as you work. Press all seams towards the darkest color after each step.

1. For the left border, arrange the five peach triangles on the gunmetal brown. Remove the paper backing from the triangles and bond the two together. Appliqué the sides of the triangles using narrow satin stitch.

2. For the top border, stitch the aubergine and gunmetal brown strips together. Arrange two peach triangles and three wine red triangles on the strip so that one wine red triangle covers the join of the two background fabrics. Bond and appliqué the triangle sides using narrow satin stitch.

3. From the bright red corduroy, cut one house roof. Cut one square 1½ × 1½ in / 3.8 × 3.8 cm for the top right corner. Cut one rectangle 2 × 1½ in / 5.1 × 3.8 cm for the right border.

4. From the cherry red corduroy, cut one house side.

5. From the soft red, cut four triangles for the bottom border. Cut one rectangular shape 2½ × 2¾ in / 6.4 × 7 cm for the bottom left corner. Cut one square 1 × 1 in / 2.5 × 2.5 cm for the top left corner.

6. From the wine red, cut three triangles for the bottom border and three triangles for the top border.

7. From the aubergine, cut one strip 8 × 2 in / 20.3 × 5.1 cm for the bottom border. Cut one strip 6 × 2 in / 15.2 × 5.1 cm for the top border.

8. From the royal blue, cut two squares 1¼ × 1¼ in / 3.2 × 3.2 cm for the bottom right and left corners. Cut one strip 2 × 1¾ in / 5.1 × 4.5 cm for the top left corner. Cut one strip 2 × ¾ in / 5.1 × 1.9 cm for the right border.

9. From the gunmetal brown, cut one strip 5¾ × 2 in / 14.6 × 5.1 cm for the top border. Cut one strip 4 × 2 in / 10.2 × 5.1 cm for the bottom border.

3. For the right border, stitch the bright red corduroy rectangle between the two pieces of gunmetal brown to make a strip 10½ × 2 in / 26.7 × 5.1 cm. Position the royal blue rectangle at the top of the strip and bond in position. Cut one peach triangle in half from the top to the center base and arrange the five triangles and two half triangles on the background strip. Bond and appliqué the triangle sides and the royal blue rectangle sides.

4. For the bottom border, stitch the aubergine and gunmetal brown strips together. Cut in half one soft red triangle and one wine red triangle from top point to center base. Discard two half triangles. Arrange three and a half soft red triangles and two and a half wine red triangles on the background so that one wine red triangle covers the join.

5. For the bottom left corner, bond the royal blue square to the soft red square. For the bottom right corner, bond the royal blue square to the gunmetal brown square. For the top left corner, bond the bright red corduroy square to the peach rectangle. For the top right corner, bond the soft red square to the royal blue square and the royal blue square to the gunmetal brown square. Satin stitch around the inner raw edges.

6. Arrange the borders and corners on the right side of the cushion front, ½ in / 1.3 cm in from the raw edges. Bond and appliqué in place.

7. To make the house motif, bond the windows to the house front and side and satin stitch around the raw edges. Arrange the house roof, front and side in the center of the cushion front, so that the roof overlaps the front and side, and the side overlaps the house front. Bond and appliqué around the raw edges.

8. To make the cushion, turn under ⅜ in / 1 cm on one 17 in / 43.2 cm edge of the piece measuring 16½ × 17 in / 41.9 × 43.2 cm. Turn under a further 1¼ in / 3.2 cm and press. On the right side of the fabric, work a row of stitching close to the hemmed edge and a second row 1 in / 2.5 cm away. Repeat on one 17 in / 43.2 cm edge of the 5 × 17 in / 12.7 × 43.2 cm length. Make three buttonholes equal

distances apart on the hemmed edge of the larger piece. Stitch three buttons on the shorter piece to align with the buttonholes.

9. Lay the pieces out on a clean, flat surface. With right sides face up, overlap the hemmed edge of the larger piece over the hemmed edge of the small piece until the length of the whole measures 16 in / 40.6 cm. Stitch together the overlap at each side.

10. With right sides facing, stitch the cushion front to the cushion back allowing ½ in / 1.3 cm seam. Turn right side out and insert the cushion pad into the cover. If you are using a bought cushion pad, shake the filling down and sew a 1 in / 2.5 cm seam along one side. Trim the excess away.

HARE AND HOUSE RUG

SIZE 35½ × 33 in / 90.2 × 83.8 cm

MATERIALS

■ All measurements are based on a fabric width of 45 in / 114.3 cm.

18 in / 46 cm square purple washable felt

18 in / 46 cm square black washable felt

¼ yd / 0.25 m bottle green wool

¼ yd / 0.25 m wine colored wool

¼ yd / 0.25 m bright red flannel for the hares

¼ yd / 0.25 m terracotta corduroy for the tree tops

¼ yd / 0.25 m black cotton for the appliqué border and side binding

Scraps of flannel and felt for the base of the tree, house and appliqué border motifs

1 yd / 1 m fusible webbing

1 yd / 1 m tearaway stabilizer

1 yd / 1 m pelmet-weight Vilene

¾ yd / 0.7 m of 2 oz / 50 gm batting

1 yd / 1 m strong cotton backing

CUTTING

■ Before cutting, dampen all wool and corduroy fabrics and iron dry to prevent shrinkage when washing. Read the General Techniques chapter for instructions on making templates, using fusible webbing, and appliqué.

1. Cut each felt square in half lengthways to make four 9 × 18 in / 22.9 × 45.7 cm rectangles. Stitch the two black rectangles together to make one strip 9 × 36 in / 22.9 × 91.4 cm. Repeat stitching the purple felt rectangles in the same way.

2. Cut the bottle green wool to measure 9 × 36 in / 22.9 × 91.4 cm.

3. Cut the wine colored wool to measure 9 × 36 in / 22.9 × 91.4 cm.

4. From appropriate colors bond and cut right and left facing hares, tree tops, trunks, sprigs and houses.

5. For the appliqué border, cut two strips across the width of the black cotton 2½ in / 6.4 cm wide.

6. From fabric scraps bond and cut rectangles 5 × 2 in / 12.7 × 5.1 cm and 1 × 2 in / 2.5 × 5.1 cm for the top and bottom border. Placed end to end the 2 in / 5.1 cm pieces should make a strip 2 yd / 182.8 cm long.

7. For the black binding, cut two strips 1¼ in / 3.2 cm wide across the fabric at a 45° angle.

MAKING UP

■ Use a ¼ in / 0.6 cm seam allowance throughout. Pin and baste each step before stitching. Trim and tidy the seam allowances as you work. Press all seams towards the darkest color after each step.

1. For the pieced rug top, stitch the black felt to the wine color, the wine color to the purple felt, and the purple felt to the bottle green, to make a rectangle 34½ × 36 in / 87.6 × 91.4 cm.

2. Position the appliqué shapes. Remove the paper backing from the fusible webbing and bond each in place.

3. Before sewing the shapes to the background, place the sheet of tearaway stabilizer underneath the felt rug to stop puckers appearing when stitching. Pin to hold. Machine appliqué using narrow satin stitch around the raw edge of each shape, then tear away the excess stabilizer.

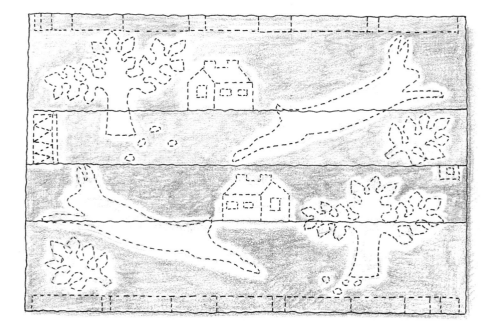

5. To make up the rug, trim the backing 2 in / 5.1 cm larger than the front at the top and bottom. Trim the sides, the batting and Vilene to the same size as the rug top. Spread the backing fabric out right side down on a clean, flat surface. Center the Vilene on top, then the batting and the rug front. Baste the layers together horizontally, vertically, diagonally and along each edge.

6. To self-bind the top and bottom only of the rug, read page 108 of the General Techniques chapter.

7. To bind the two sides using single-fold binding, fold the binding in half lengthways so that wrong sides are facing and press. Turn under one long edge and press. Align the raw edge of the binding with the raw edge of the front rug side and machine stitch in place. Fold the binding back over the stitching line to the back of the rug and press. Slipstitch the folded edge to finish.

4. To make up the rug border, appliqué the rectangles to the border strip in a random manner, leaving ¼ in / 0.6 cm seam at each edge. Appliqué around each raw edge. Stitch each border to the top and bottom of the rug.

43

The GARDEN ROOM

For The Garden Room I have chosen to represent the airy sophistication of a bygone era with stylized floral motifs, vines, ivy leaves, bees, butterflies and snails. Soft white, cream, leafy greens and delicate mauves combine to create a cool ambience in a flower-filled paradise – an ideal place of retreat on a hot summer's day or somewhere to chase away the winter blues. Adapt any of the floral motifs from the wallhanging or tablecloth to personalize throws cushions, or chair covers.

VINE AND IVY LEAF TABLECLOTH

SIZE 65 in / 165.1 cm square

■ The four central squares of the Vine and Ivy Leaf Tablecloth are made using reverse appliqué. The floral motifs on the outer squares are applied using raw edge appliqué. The four squares in the bottom left corner make one pattern. The remaining blocks of four squares are mirror images of this block.

MATERIALS

■ All measurements are based on a fabric width of 45 in / 114.3 cm except where stated otherwise.

2 yd / 1.9 m of 90 in / 228 cm wide white cotton sheeting

2 yd / 1.9 m turquoise for the squares

1½ yd / 1.4 m mid-green for the borders and binding

18 in / 46 cm square each of dark green, light green, blue-green, purple, lilac, brick red, and light brown for the appliqué motifs

Scraps of yellow for the flower centers

8 yd / 7.3 m fusible webbing

2 yd / 1.9 m tearaway stabilizer

Two small flat beads for eyes

Embroidery floss for the bee

CUTTING

■ Wash all fabrics separately first. Read the General Techniques chapter for instructions on using fusible webbing, making templates, enlarging a grid, and appliqué.

1. Make templates for each of the appliqué shapes. Enlarge the grid for the vine pattern, following the instructions on page 105.

2. From the white cotton sheeting, cut one square 64 × 64 in / 162.6 × 162.6 cm.

3. For the binding, cut two strips 3¾ × 64 in / 9.5 × 162.6 cm, and two strips 3¾ × 72 in / 9.5 × 182.9 cm.

4. Bond fusible webbing to the reverse of the turquoise fabric and cut 16 squares each 12 × 12 in / 30.5 × 30.5 cm. Center the large flower template on each of four squares and draw around the shape using a fabric marker pen. Carefully cut out the flower, without cutting the border.

5. From the dark green, for the border bond and cut eight strips 12 ×

1 in / 30.5 × 2.5 cm. Bond and cut four corner borders 1 in / 2.5 cm wide, use a turquoise square as your guide.

6. From the remaining fabrics, bond and cut out the required number of each of the appliqué shapes using your templates, and remembering to reverse the templates where necessary.

MAKING UP

■ Use a ¼ in / 0.6 cm seam allowance throughout. Pin and baste each step before stitching. Trim and tidy the seam allowances as you work. Press all seams towards the darkest color.

1. To give guidelines to position the 16 turquoise squares, fold the tablecloth in half and then into quarters. Press lightly with a hot iron. Open out and spread out on a clean flat surface. Position the four squares with the cut-out flower motif in the center of the tablecloth, ½ in / 1.3 cm to each side of the pressed guidelines.

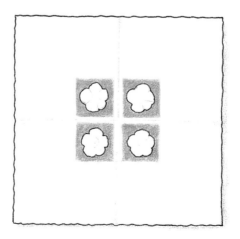

This is the artist's original design. It has been simplified to make each quarter symmetrical.

Remove the paper backing from the fusible webbing and bond each in position. Place a sheet of tearaway stabilizer behind your work before stitching to prevent puckers from appearing. Pin in position. Appliqué around the raw edges of the flower and the turquoise square, changing colors where necessary and taking care not to catch the pins.

2. Trace the details of the flower petals from the pattern, and transfer the tracing to the tablecloth by aligning your tracing with the cut out shape from the turquoise square. Rub over the tracings with a pencil. The traced lines will provide the stitching line for the flower details. Stitch over the pencil lines using narrow satin stitch to create the flower details.

6. Re-position the vines on each of the squares within your marked guidelines. Overlap slightly the light green leaf over the vine. Place the tendrils just under the vine in each of the four corners. When you are happy with the arrangement remove the paper backing and fuse each in place using a hot iron. Appliqué around each raw edge using narrow satin stitch.

3. Fuse a yellow center to each of the four flowers. Appliqué the raw edges.

4. Measure and mark with pins the position of the twelve remaining turquoise squares around the center four with a 1 in / 2.5 cm border of white tablecloth showing between the squares. Pin in position. When you are happy with the arrangement, fuse the squares to the white cloth. Position the dark green border pieces and corners on top of the turquoise squares so that outer raw edges are aligned. Fuse the layers together, then appliqué around each raw edge.

5. Build up the appliqué motifs in the following order. Position the vines on each of the squares and mark their position as a guide to placing each of the leaves, then remove the stems. Position the eight blue-green and eight light green leaves on eight of the outer turquoise squares, avoiding the corner pieces. Pin the eight dark green leaves to the outer edge of the tablecloth, so that they just overlap the dark green border.

7. Position the corner flowers, placing the purple background petals of the flower before the lilac center petals.

8. Finally, position the bee and snail and the markings on each body. Using matching sewing thread and changing colors where necessary, appliqué around each of the motifs so that the line of stitching covers the raw edges of each shape. Machine satin stitch the details of the snail's shell and the bee's body. Hand stitch the legs and antennae of the bee using stem stitch (See page 112). Stitch the flat beads on for eyes.

9. To bind the edges of the tablecloth using single-fold binding, fold each length of binding in half lengthways so that wrong sides are facing and press. Open out the binding. Turn in ½ in / 1.3 cm seam allowance on one of the long raw edges to the pressed foldline and press. Using the 64 in / 162.6 cm lengths of binding, and with right sides facing, align the raw edge of the binding with the raw edge of the left-hand side of the tablecloth. Machine straight stitch 1 in / 2.5 cm from the edge of the tablecloth. Fold the binding over to the back of the tablecloth and press. Slipstitch the folded edge in place. Repeat this step stitching the second length of binding to the right-hand side, then the two 72 in / 182.9 cm lengths to the top and bottom. Press to finish.

APPLIQUÉ FLOWER CUSHION

SIZE 16 in / 40.1 cm square

MATERIALS

■ All measurements are based on a fabric width of 45 in / 114.3 cm except where stated otherwise.

½ yd / 0.5 m white cotton for the cushion front and back

18 × 22 in / 46 × 56 cm jade-green cotton to cover the piping cord

12 in / 30 cm square contrast color for the flower motif

Scraps for the bee and flower center

2 yd / 1.8 m no 3 piping cord

16 in / 40 cm square cushion pad

16 in / 40 cm nylon zip

CUTTING

■ Wash all your fabrics separately before cutting to ensure that they are colorfast. Read the General Techniques chapter for instructions on using fusible webbing, making templates, and appliqué.

1. For the cushion front, from the white cotton, cut one square 16½ × 16½ in / 41.9 × 41.9 cm. Cut the same for the cushion back.

2. Make templates for each motif. Trace onto the flower template each petal outline. Bond and cut one flower from the contrasting color, one flower center, and one bee from different colored fabric scraps.

3. For covering the piping cord, use the jade-green fabric and cut strips 1½ in / 3.8 cm wide.

MAKING UP

■ Use a ¼ in / 0.6 cm seam allowance throughout. Pin and baste each step before stitching. Trim and tidy the seam allowances as you work. Press all seams towards the darkest color after each step.

1. Remove the paper backing from the appliqué motifs and fuse each to the cushion front. Appliqué around the raw edges and satin stitch the details.

2. To make 2¼ yd / 2.1 m of continuous binding for covering the piping cord and to pipe the edges of the cushion front, read the instructions on page 108 and for the Cowboy Bolster Cushion on page 96.

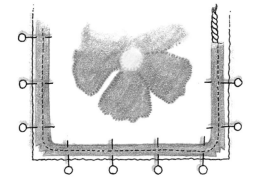

3. To insert the zip, position the cushion front right side up on a clean, flat surface. At the bottom of the cushion, place the zip, right side down and with the zip tab to the left. Baste in position. Using a zipper foot, machine stitch down one side of the zip close to the piping cord, taking care not to catch the teeth of the zip.

Align the right side of the cushion back with the cushion front and machine stitch down the other side of the zip ¼ in / 0.6 cm from the raw edge of the cushion back.

4. Part open the zip. Align the corners and raw edges of the cushion front and back and baste in place close to the piping. Machine stitch around each of the remaining three sides close to the piping.

5. Machine overcast the raw edges at the bottom of the cushion at each side of the zip. Machine overcast the raw edges of the three sides of the front and back cushion together. Turn right side out and insert the cushion pad.

BUTTERFLY WALLHANGING

SIZE 33 in / 83.8 cm square

MATERIALS

■ All measurements are based on a fabric width of 45 in / 114.3 cm except where stated otherwise.

2 yd / 2 m cream cotton for the front and backing

1 yd / 1 m sage green cotton for the border

½ yd / 0.5 m small blue print for binding

18 × 22 in / 46 × 56 cm each of dark green, lilac, purple, shocking pink, light pink, light blue, royal blue, dark coral, and light coral for the appliqué motifs

Scraps for the butterfly, snail and bee

33 × 33 in / 84 × 84 cm of 2 oz / 50 gm batting

1½ yd / 1.4 m fusible webbing

1 yd / 1 m tearaway stabilizer

One skein embroidery floss for the tendrils

1 yd / 1 m thin hanging cord

32 × 1⅝ in / 81 × 4 cm wooden dowel for hanging

CUTTING

■ Wash all your fabrics separately before cutting. Read the General Techniques chapter for instructions on using fusible webbing, making templates, enlarging a grid, and machine appliqué.

1. Make templates from the patterns provided. Enlarge the grid.

2. From the cream cotton for the front and backing of the wallhanging, cut two squares each 33 × 33 in / 83.8 × 83.8 cm. For the appliqué border and vine cut one square 33 × 33 in / 83.8 × 83.8 cm from the sage green.

3. From the remaining cream cotton, cut one length 5 × 31 in / 12.7 × 78.7 cm for the hanging sleeve.

4. Bond and cut each appliqué motif from the appropriate color fabric. Label each piece as you work.

5. For the separate binding, from the small blue print, cut four lengths 2½ in / 6.4 cm wide across the width of the fabric.

6. Cut one square 23 × 23 in / 58.4 × 58.4 cm of fusible webbing.

MAKING UP

■ The sage green border and vine is cut out and applied to the cream cotton in one single piece. Use a ¼ in / 0.6 cm seam allowance throughout. Pin and baste each step before stitching. Trim and tidy the seam allowances as you work.

1. For the vine and border, on the wrong side of the sage green cotton, measure and mark a border 5 in / 12.7 cm from the raw edges using a fabric marker pen. Using a hot iron, bond the 23 in / 58.4 cm square of fusible webbing to the center of the

sage green, so that the edges meet the marked border lines. Do not remove the paper backing at this stage.

2. Place your vine template right side down in the center of the bonded square. Mark an outline.

With small, pointed, sharp scissors, carefully cut out the vine shape, leaving the border in place and in one piece. Remove the paper backing.

3. On a clean, flat surface, spread out the cream cotton for the front right side up. On top center the green border and vine pattern, remove the paper backing and bond the two together.

4. Bond each of the dark green leaves in place. Then bond the butterfly, flowers, bud, bee and snail. Place a sheet of tearaway stabilizer behind the wallhanging to stop puckers appearing when stitching.

5. Using matching threads and changing where necessary, machine appliqué over each raw edge. Remove the tearaway stabilizer.

6. Using a fabric marker, draw in the tendrils, and using three strands of embroidery floss stem stitch (See page 112) to fill in each shape. The bee's and the snail's eyes are made using one French knot (See page 112). The legs and antennae are worked in just one row of stem stitch.

7. Using the remaining cream square for backing, make up the quilt sandwich. On a clean, flat surface, spread the backing out right side down. On top center the batting, then the top right side up. Baste the three layers together horizontally, vertically and around the edges. Trim all raw edges even.

8. Hand quilt with running stitch around the outline of the flowers, butterfly and stem. Echo quilt the outer edge of the cream square ¼ in / 0.6 cm from the green border. Hand quilt a straight line in the center of the green border.

9. To make single-fold binding and to bind the wallhanging, follow the instructions for separate binding on pages 109 and 110.

10. To make a hanging sleeve, turn under a small seam allowance at each of the short ends and machine stitch to hold. Fold the strip in half lengthways and stitch the two raw edges together. Turn the sleeve right side out and press so that the seam is in the center back. Slipstitch the hanging sleeve to the top of the wallhanging, (so that the seam does not show).

11. To complete, drill a hole in each end of the wooden dowel and thread hanging cord through the holes. Knot in the middle.

The
DINING
ROOM

A thirties-style scene of rural domestic-
ity is recreated in this striking and
unusual design. Reminiscent of scenes
painted by pottery artist Clarice Cliff
the bushes and trees are clipped and
manicured, the flora and fauna are
neat and tidy. I have chosen bright and
bold colors in plain cotton fabrics to
emphasize the crisp lines of this country landscape. The striking color
scheme, reminiscent of the Art Deco
period and light-hearted motifs will
brighten the mood of any room.

DINING CHAIR BACK COVERS

SIZE 25 × 15 in / 63.5 × 38.1 cm
adapt the pattern as necessary

MATERIALS

■ All measurements are based on a fabric width of 45 in / 114.3 cm. The list supplied below is for the cobalt blue chair back cover only.

27 × 60 in / 0.7 × 1.5 m cobalt blue cotton for the background

18 × 22 in / 46 × 56 cm white cotton for the cloud

18 × 22 in / 46 × 56 cm marigold yellow cotton for the hill

18 × 22 in / 46 × 56 cm bright orange cotton for the hill and trees

18 × 22 in / 46 × 56 cm terracotta cotton for the roof, hill and tree

18 × 22 in / 46 × 56 cm wine cotton for the bushes

18 × 22 in / 46 × 56 cm apricot cotton for the house

Scraps of black cotton for the windows

½ yd / 0.5 m fusible webbing

½ yd / 0.5 m tearaway stabilizer

½ yd / 0.5 m of 2 oz / 50 gm polyester batting

¾ yd / 0.7 m muslin for backing

Cotton perlé embroidery thread

CUTTING

■ Before cutting, dampen all wool and corduroy fabrics and iron dry to prevent shrinkage when washing. Read the General Techniques chapter for instructions on making templates, using fusible webbing, and appliqué.

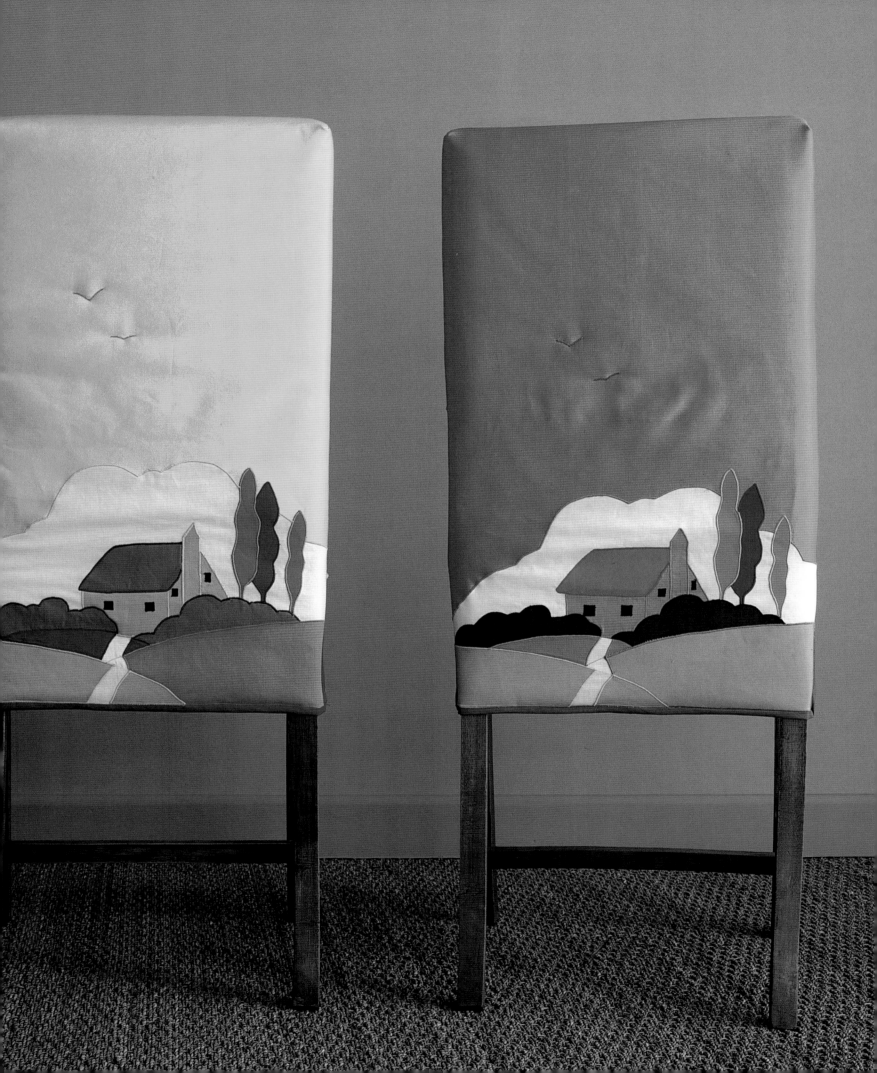

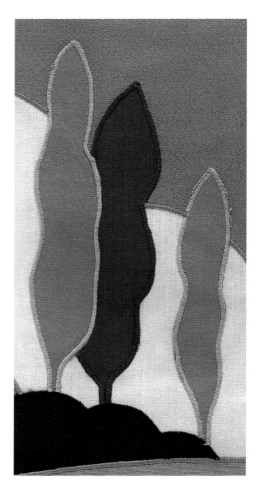

1. Make templates for each of the appliqué shapes. Cut each shape from the appropriate color fabric. Use your templates and cut slightly larger shapes from fusible webbing. Put the cloud shape to one side, then bond the webbing to the reverse of every other motif. Cut the paper backing to the exact size.

2. For the chair cover, from cobalt blue, cut one length 46½ × 18 in / 118.1 × 45.7 cm. Cut the batting and the backing to the same size.

3. To make the continuous binding for the bottom edges of the chair cover, from the remaining cobalt blue cut one piece 27 × 13½ in / 68.6 × 34.2 cm and from this cut strips 1½ in / 3.8 cm wide and follow the instructions in the General Techniques chapter on page 108.

MAKING UP

■ Use a ¼ in / 0.6 cm seam allowance throughout. Pin and baste each step before stitching. Trim and tidy the seam allowances as you work. Press all seams towards the darkest color after each step.

1. Trace the position of the house, hills, bushes and trees on the white cloud. Leave the three tall trees until the cloud has been bonded to the chair back. When you are happy with the arrangement, fuse each in place in the order shown in the illustration. Build up the design by applying all the shapes which are overlapped and in the background first.

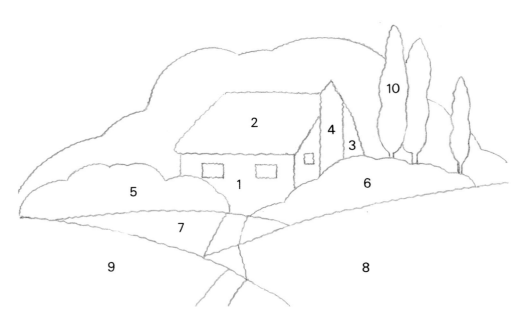

2. Place a sheet of tearaway stabilizer behind the bonded shapes and using narrow satin stitch and changing colored threads where necessary, appliqué around each raw edge. Define the pathway with machine straight stitch. When each piece is applied tear away the stabilizer. Press carefully.

3. Bond fusible webbing to the reverse of the cloud, then position the picture at one end of the chair back. Fuse in place. Fuse the three tall trees to the right-hand side of the design. Machine appliqué each raw edge.

4. To layer the chair back, place the backing right side down on a clean, flat surface. On top center the batting, then the chair back design right side up. Baste each of the layers together. Trim all raw edges even.

5. Using stem stitch (See page 112) embroider the two birds to the design. The birds will act as holding stitches.

6. Fold the chair back in half across the width, right sides facing and with raw edges aligned. Measure and mark a point 5½ in / 14 cm from the bottom of each side seam. Stitch the side seams together from the top to the marked 5½ in / 14 cm point. Press the seams open.

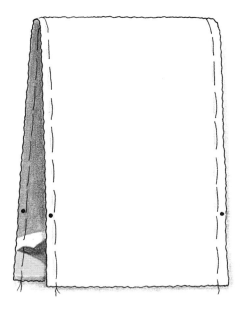

7. To make the side panels of the chair back, with the side seam facing you, near the fold at the top, with each hand separate the back and front, pulling the folded top edge down and out, to make a triangle shape at the

top of the side seam. Measure and mark 1 in / 2.5 cm from the top of the side seam and stitch a horizontal line 2 in / 5.1 cm long across the top of the triangle. Reinforce the stitching.

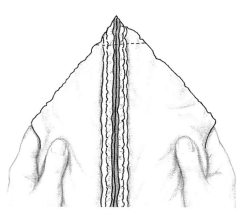

8. To make up 3 yd / 3 m of continuous binding for the side flaps, bottom edge of the chair back, and for ties, follow the instructions for double-fold binding in the General Techniques chapter. Bind the raw edges of the sides. Center the binding along each bottom edge so that there is 12 in / 30.5 cm of binding at each end to make the ties. With right sides together align the raw edge of the binding with the raw edge of the chair back and stitch on the first foldline. Turn the binding into the inside of the chair back and slipstitch to secure. Machine stitch the folded edges of the binding together for the ties.

ART DECO WALLHANGING

SIZE 30 × 43 in / 76.2 × 109.2 cm

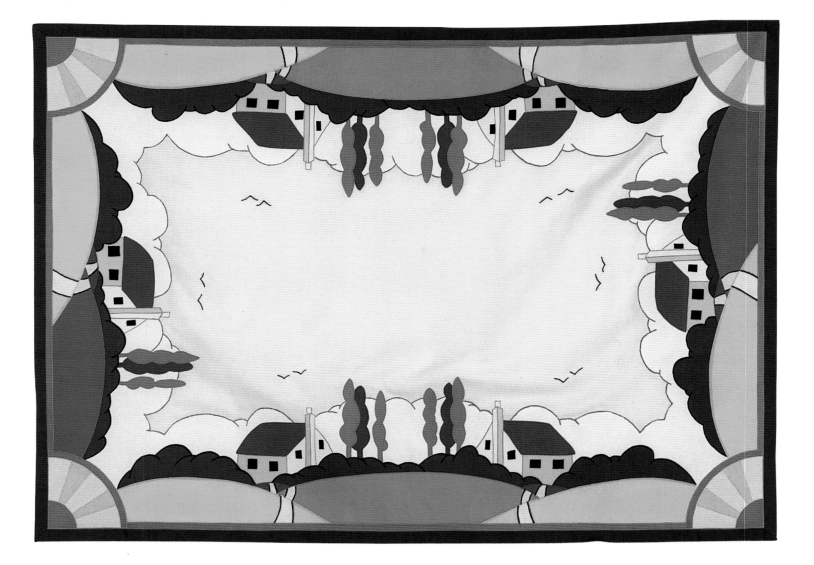

MATERIALS

■ All measurements are based on a fabric width of 45 in / 114.3 cm.

1 yd / 1 m cream cotton for the background and house side

18 × 22 in / 46 × 56 cm taupe for the landscape

18 × 22 in / 46 × 56 cm turquoise

7 × 10 in / 18 × 25 cm medium-brown

½ yd / 0.5 m dark-brown for the binding

⅓ yd / 0.3 m orange for the border and corners

5 in / 13 cm square black for the windows

18 × 22 in / 46 × 56 cm sunflower yellow for the sunrays and landscape

12 × 18 in / 30 × 46 cm lavender for the trees

6 × 12 in / 15 × 30 cm purple for the trees

12 in / 30 cm square russet for the roof

10 × 12 in / 25 × 30 cm salmon pink for the house front and chimney

¼ yd / 0.25 m cobalt blue for the shrubs

1 yd / 1 m white for the clouds, pathways, corner motif, and sunrays

1 yd / 1 m backing fabric

3½ yd / 3.1 m fusible webbing

6 × 40 in / 15 × 100 cm cotton for the hanging sleeve

1 yd / 1 m length wooden batten

CUTTING

■ Before cutting, wash all fabrics and iron dry without stretching or distorting fabric. Read the General Techniques chapter for instructions on making templates, enlarging a grid, using fusible webbing, appliqué, and double-fold binding. Pad a large, flat surface for use when pinning and bonding the design motifs to the cream cotton. Use two old blankets and a double thickness of sheeting on a large, flat surface. Smooth out all the layers so that there are no wrinkles and pin tightly at the corners to ensure the surface will not slip. The cloud template contains the upper outlines of the house and the trees, this will help to ensure accurate placement of all pattern pieces.

1. Enlarge the grid for the wallhanging following the instructions on page 105. Make a mastercopy and keep it as a guide for pattern placement. Do not cut the mastercopy. Make your own templates for each of the motifs.

2. For the back of the wallhanging cut one piece 32 × 45 in / 81.3 × 114.3 cm. Ensure the corners are right angles.

3. For the front of the wallhanging, cut one piece 32 × 45 in / 81.3 × 114.3 cm. Fold in half lengthways and press lightly to find the center line. Fold in half crossways to find the center of the long sides. Make sure that each of the corners are true right angles and trim accordingly.

4. Trace all the motifs on the paper side of the fusible webbing. First cut out the cloud template. Although the cloud forms a continuous border, cut the cloud in six pieces. The cutting lines follow the lines of the chimneys. The cloud template contains the upper outline of the houses and trees. This will ensure accurate placement of the smaller pattern pieces. Rough cut around each and bond to the appropriate fabric. Once the fabric is bonded pin the paper backing and bonded fabric together in case the paper slips. Refer to the templates to determine where extra fabric is necessary for overlapping. When cutting add ⅛ in / 0.3 cm to the motifs that will be overlapped. Finally, accurately cut out each fabric piece and set aside.

5. Bond and cut four corner arcs from orange to back the sunrays.

6. For the brown continuous binding, trim selvages off the dark brown fabric and cut four strips 3 in / 7.6 cm wide across the width of the fabric.

7. For the orange border, bond and cut one strip 2½ × 41 in / 6.4 × 104.1 cm, and from this cut two strips ½ × 41 in / 1.3 × 104.1 cm, and two strips ½ × 28 in / 1.3 × 71.1 cm.

MAKING UP

1. Spread the cream backing out on your prepared surface and smooth out any wrinkles. To mark the finished size of the wallhanging draw a guideline 1 in / 2.5 cm in from each raw edge. Draw a second guideline 2 in / 5.1 cm in from each raw edge. This is your guide for placing all the template pieces.

2. To make up the corner motifs, to the orange corner areas bond and appliqué alternate yellow and white rays ¼ in / 0.6 cm from the raw curved edges and the side edges.

This is the artist's original design. Change the color scheme to suit your own palette.

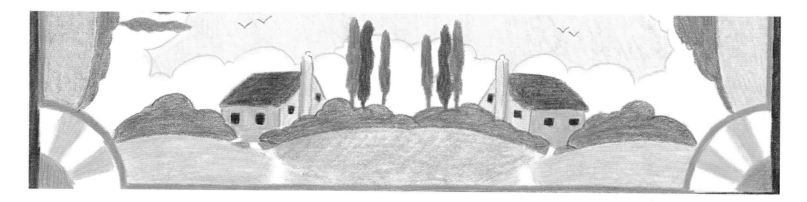

3. Build up the design in the following order. Pin the yellow, turquoise and taupe landscape pieces in position so that they overlap by ⅛ in / 0.3 cm the marked 2 in / 5.1 cm guideline. Then position and pin the cloud so that it tucks in behind the landscape. Smooth out any wrinkles.

4. Pin on the white pathways, the cobalt blue shrubbery, and the corners. Adjust all the pieces until every motif is in the correct place and there are no raw edges showing from underneath. Mark with a light pencil the outline of each on the background to make repositioning easier.

5. When each is positioned, one at a time carefully remove the landscape pieces. Bond and appliqué the pathway using black thread. Re-position each landscape piece. This will ensure you do not disturb the final placement. Bond and appliqué the black windows to the houses.

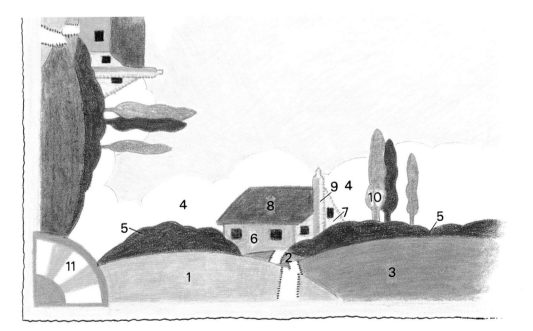

6. Bond the lower part of the landscape pieces only – approximately 1 in / 2.5 cm along each edge. This will hold everything in place so that you can begin to add the more detailed pattern pieces. Add the house pieces and trees.

7. Tuck the bottom of the house under the line of the shrubbery and pathways and the bottom of the tree trunks under the line of the shrubbery. You should have no difficulty placing the trees as the base outline is already included in the cloud template.

8. Once all the motifs are in place work methodically to bond the pieces, only removing the pins when you are sure that the pattern pieces will not slip out of position.

9. Add the orange border, aligning each strip with the bottom of the landscape and overlapping the landscape pieces by ⅛ in / 0.3 cm. Add the corner sun motifs overlapping the cloud and shrubbery. Draw in any detail lines using a pencil, such as the clouds and chimney.

10. Appliqué each raw edge. Use narrow satin stitch to define the chimney. Both matching and contrasting thread have been used throughout to provide an outline for

the pieces. Contrasting thread appliqué requires greater skill than working with matching thread, but enhances the period look of the design.

11. Embroider the birds on the background fabric in chain stitch or stem stitch (See page 112) using four strands of embroidery floss.

12. Press the wallhanging. Spread the backing out right side down. Place the appliqué design on top right side up. Pin and baste the layers together and trim any excess backing away.

13. Bind the wallhanging with the dark brown continuous binding, sewing mitered corners as you work. Slipstitch close the miters.

14. Follow the instructions for the Butterfly Wallhanging on page 55 to make a hanging sleeve.

CLARICE CLIFF DRAPES

SIZE 48 × 80 in / 121.9 × 203.2 cm long

■ Directions are given for the left-hand drape of the pair only. Reverse the pattern pieces for the right-hand side of the pair of drapes. When enlarging the grid on a 1½ in / 3.8 cm square grid, each half of the drape will be 48 in / 122 cm wide. If each square is enlarged on a 2 in / 5.1 cm grid each half will be 64 in / 163 cm wide. Amend your grid size as necessary.

MATERIALS

For each side of the drape measuring 48 in / 122 cm wide you will need:

2⅝ yd / 2.4 m of 60 in / 152 cm wide light-blue cotton for the background

1⅔ yd / 1.5 m white for the cloud

¼ yd / 0.25 m lavender for the tree

⅓ yd / 0.3 m blue for the tree

13 × 8 in / 33 × 20 cm sunflower yellow for sunrays

13 × 8 in / 33 × 20 cm salmon for the sunrays

½ yd / 0.5 m light-wheat yellow for the landscape

½ yd / 0.5 m blue for the shrubbery

⅔ yd / 0.6 m light-brown for the tree trunk and two trees

3 × 20 in / 8 × 51 cm dark-brown for a tree

18 × 22 in / 46 × 56 cm turquoise for the pathway

Scrap of green

Scrap of orange

Scrap of black

½ yd / 0.5 m coffee brown

88 in / 223 cm of 48 in / 122 cm wide lining

12¼ yd / 11 m fusible webbing

5 × 48 in / 13 × 122 cm light-weight buckram or medium-weight interfacing

Pincer clips for the top of the drape

CUTTING

■ Read the General Techniques chapter for instructions on enlarging a grid, making templates, using fusible webbing, and appliqué. When working with large projects work on a large, clean, flat surface.

1. For each drape, measure the depth of the drop and cut the length of the drapes 10½ in / 26.7 cm longer. For a 48 in / 121.9 cm width cut the fabric 2 in / 5.1 cm wider.

2. Prepare your drape lengths. Be certain the bottom of the drape is at a true right angle to the selvage. Trim off the selvages. Draw a guideline 5 in / 12.7 cm from the bottom raw edge. This is your placement line for the pattern pieces and forms the bottom edge of the finished drape.

3. For the lining of each drape, cut one piece 48 in / 121.9 cm × the length of your drape less 2½ in / 6.4 cm. (For an 80 in / 203.2 cm length this will be 80 in / 203.2 cm + 11 in / 27.9 cm for the hems − 2½ in / 6.4 cm = 88½ in / 224.7 cm.)

4. Enlarge the grid and make templates for each of the motifs. Add ⅛ in / 0.3 cm at the points of overlap.

5. Place the templates right side down on the paper side of fusible webbing and draw an outline. Rough cut around

each shape. Cut each pattern piece from the appropriate color fabric. Using the grid as a guide, mark with pencil all the details such as clouds and windows on the right side of the fabric. Bond fusible webbing to the reverse of each shape, then cut the excess webbing away. Use baking parchment on your ironing board.

6. For the hem of the drape, cut one strip of fusible webbing 5 × 48 in /12.7 × 121.9 cm.

MAKING UP

1. Bond each of the motifs working from the hem of the drape up.

Position the landscape pieces making sure that the fabrics overlap at the joins by ⅛ in / 0.3 cm. Position the cloud and tuck the sunray in behind. Begin bonding, taking care that the pieces do not slip and that the background remains absolutely flat. Do not remove any pins until you are certain that all the pieces are bonded.

Position the shrubbery, the large tree in the foreground, the cluster of trees in the background, then the circular motifs. When you are satisfied that the pieces are correctly arranged and overlap where necessary, bond the pieces in place.

2. Machine appliqué each raw edge and define all the details using machine satin stitch. Use thread which is significantly darker than the color of the fabric shape. This will give the motifs a sharp outline and a period look to the design.

3. To make the hem of the drape, overcast the bottom raw edge, turn under 5 in / 12.7 cm at the bottom raw edge and press. Open out the fold. Place the 5 in / 12.7 cm strip of fusible webbing between the foldline and the overcast raw edge and fuse in position. Remove the paper backing and re-fold the hem in place. Fuse together.

4. Turn under 1 in / 2.5 cm at each side and press. Open out the folds.

5. To make the top of the drape, overcast the top raw edge. Turn under ½ in / 1.3 cm to the wrong side and press. Turn under a further 5 in / 12.7 cm and press. The second foldline will become the top of the drape. Open out both folds. On the wrong side of the drape, place a length of 5 in / 12.7 cm wide buckram between the two foldlines. The buckram will provide additional stability. Trim the

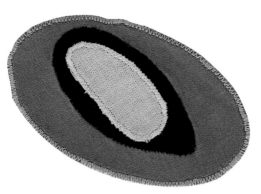

buckram at each edge so that it does not run into the seam allowance. Machine straight stitch in place.

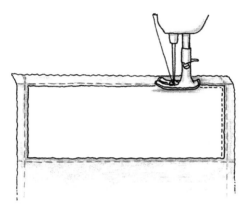

6. With right sides together re-fold the drape in the opposite direction so that the second foldline and the edge of the buckram are at the top of the drape. At each side of the top of the drape only, stitch a 1 in / 2.5 cm seam holding the hem in place.

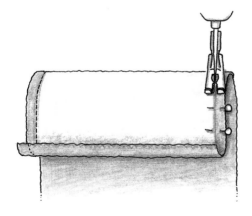

7. To make the lining, turn under ½ in / 1.3 cm at the bottom raw edge.

Further turn under 2 in / 5.1 cm to form a hem. Machine straight stitch in place. Topstitch to hold the top of the hem in position. Overcast the three remaining raw edges of the lining.

8. With right sides together align the finished bottom edge of the drape with the finished bottom edge of the lining, then shift the lining so that it sits ½ in / 1.3 cm above the bottom of the drape. Align the right-hand overcast edges. Ensure that the top of the lining meets the buckram. Pin in position, then machine stitch a ½ in / 1.3 cm seam from the bottom hem to the buckram. Repeat stitching the left-hand edges together.

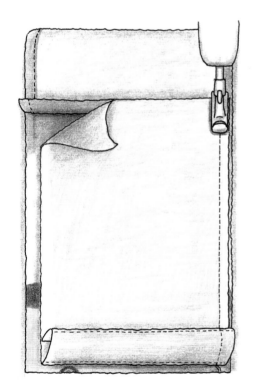

9. Slipstitch the top of the lining in position. The bottom edge of the lining will hang free of the drape. Turn the drape right side out and press carefully.

10. Clip on sufficient pincer clips at the top of the drape to align with the number of curtain rings on your curtain pole.

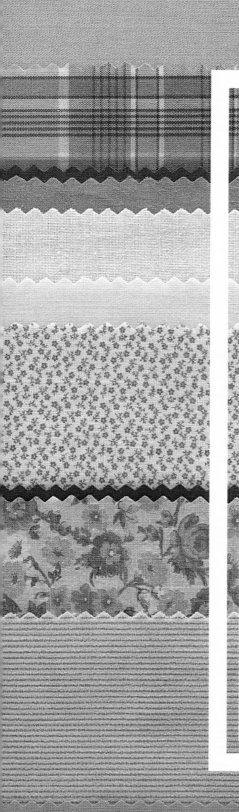

The
GIRL'S
BEDROOM

Candy shades of pastel pink and crisp white cotton are the ideal backdrop for this little girl's bedroom. Bright, fresh colors and the strong vertical stripes of the wallpaper make the room light and airy. The customized Roman blind eliminates the clutter of drapes, allowing maximum light; and the stencil motifs could be repeated to make a border around the bedroom walls or on a chest of drawers. The adorable cat motifs add character to a fun-filled quilt that a little girl will just love.

THE CONTENTED CAT QUILT

SIZE 46¾ × 61½ in / 118.8 × 156.2 cm

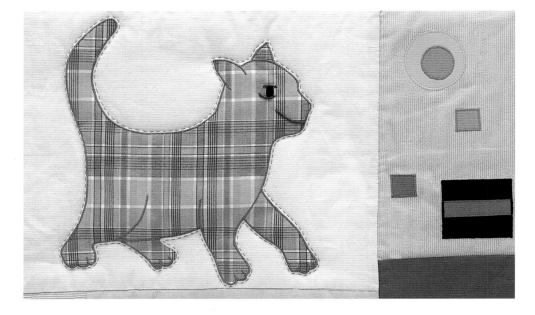

MATERIALS

■ All measurements are based on a fabric width of 45 in / 114.3 cm. 100% cotton has been used exclusively.

¾ yd / 0.7 m pale pink A

18 × 22 in / 46 × 56 cm light pink B

½ yd / 0.5 m medium pink C

⅔ yd / 0.6 m bright pink D

Scraps of small pink floral motif E

18 × 22 in / 46 × 56 cm light blue F

18 × 22 in / 46 × 56 cm bright blue G

18 × 22 in / 46 × 56 cm dark blue H

18 × 22 in / 46 × 56 cm lavender I

18 × 22 in / 46 × 56 cm light purple J

18 × 22 in / 46 × 56 cm dark purple K

18 × 22 in / 46 × 56 cm plaid for the cats L

Yellow and pink floral scraps for the initials M

18 × 22 in / 46 × 56 cm yellow N

½ yd / 0.5 m bright green O

1⅔ yd / 1.5 m white for the border and the panels P

½ yd / 0.5 m black Q

3 in / 8 cm length of 2 in / 5.1 cm wide ribbon

4 × 7 in / 10 × 18 cm fine net in a co-ordinating color

49 × 63 in / 125 × 160 cm of 2 oz/50 gm polyester batting

49 × 63 in / 125 × 160 cm backing

⅔ yd / 0.6 m of pale pink bias binding to bind the pocket

6¼ yd / 5.75 m good quality binding for the quilt or ⅓ yd / 0.3 m of fabric of your choice to make continuous binding

A selection of buttons in assorted sizes in a variety of colors for the flower centers and button-down flower flap. Small buttons for the cats' eyes

Scraps for the yo-yos

Stranded embroidery thread

2 yd / 2 m fusible webbing

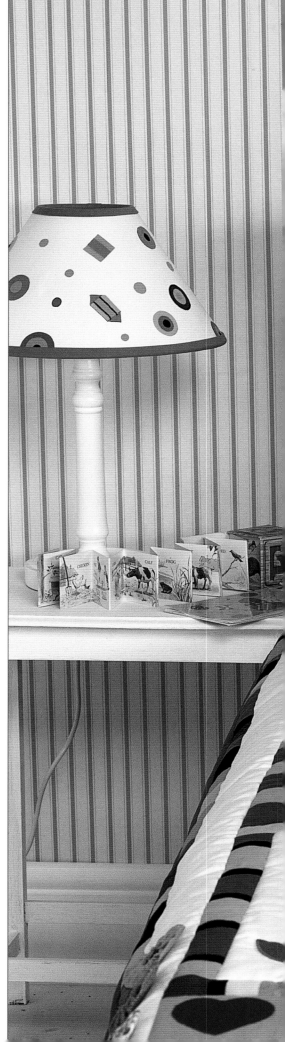

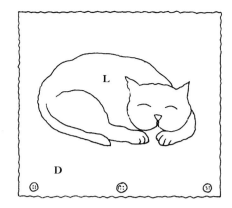

The Sleeping Cat above is the cat which sits underneath the flower flap on the right-hand side of the quilt. Below his feet is a treasure pocket, a safe haven for the tooth waiting for the tooth fairy.

■ The quilt top is made up of sections which are pieced together into panels. Each panel is then stitched together. Use the black and white line illustration as a guide.

CUTTING

■ Read the General Techniques chapter for instructions on making templates, enlarging a gird, using fusible webbing and appliqué. Label each piece with each measurement and section as you cut, and keep each section separate. Cut the largest measurements from your fabric first.

1. From pale pink A, for section 3, cut one square $3\frac{1}{2} \times 3\frac{1}{2}$ in / 8.9×8.9 cm. Cut one strip 2×5 in / 5.1×12.7 cm. For section 4, cut one rectangle $9\frac{3}{4} \times 13$ in / 24.8×33 cm. Cut one strip $1\frac{3}{4} \times 3\frac{1}{2}$ in / 4.5×8.9 cm. Bond and cut one heart.
For section 6, cut one square $14\frac{1}{2} \times 14\frac{1}{2}$ in / 36.8×36.8 cm.
For section 11, bond and cut one heart.
For section 12, cut one rectangle $16\frac{1}{2} \times 17\frac{1}{2}$ in / 41.9×44.5 cm.

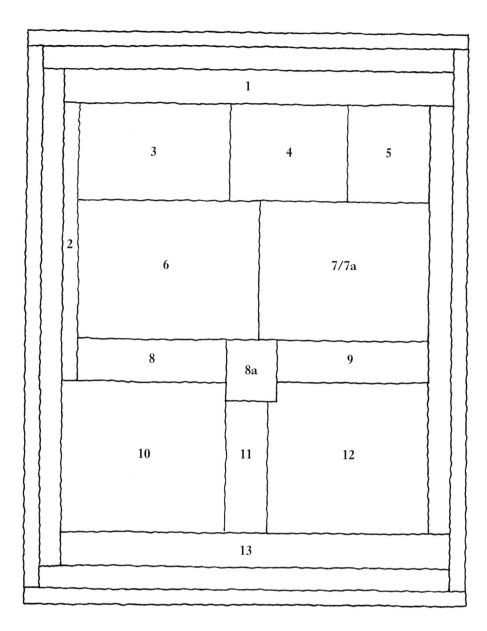

2. From light pink B, for section 3, cut two squares 2×2 in / 5.1×5.1 cm, and two rectangles $2 \times 2\frac{1}{4}$ in / 5.1×5.7 cm.
For section 4, cut one rectangle $1\frac{3}{4} \times 10$ in / 4.5×25.4 cm.
For section 5, cut one rectangle $8\frac{3}{4} \times 9\frac{1}{2}$ in / 22.2×24.1 cm.
For section 6, cut one rectangle $14\frac{1}{2} \times 1\frac{1}{2}$ in / 36.8×3.8 cm.
For section 10, cut one strip 2×8 in / 5.1×20.3 cm.
For section 11, cut one rectangle 5×6 in / 12.7×15.2 cm.

3. From medium pink C, for section 1, cut five squares each $4\frac{1}{4} \times 4\frac{1}{4}$ in / 10.8

$\times 10.8$ cm. Cut the same for section 13.
For section 2, cut seven squares $2\frac{1}{4} \times 2\frac{1}{4}$ in / 5.7×5.7 cm.
For section 3, cut one square $3\frac{1}{2} \times 3\frac{1}{2}$ in / 8.9×8.9 cm. Cut one square 2×2 in / 5.1×5.1 cm. Cut one rectangle $2 \times 2\frac{1}{4}$ in / 5.1×5.7 cm.
For section 4, cut one rectangle $4 \times 4\frac{1}{2}$ in / 10.2×11.4 cm.
For section 6, cut one rectangular shape $4\frac{1}{2} \times 5\frac{1}{2}$ in / 11.4×14 cm. Bond and cut one rectangle $1\frac{3}{4} \times 3$ in / 4.5×7.6 cm.
For section 7a cut three rectangular shapes $2\frac{3}{4} \times 4$ in / 7×10.2 cm (half will be used in section 10). Bond and cut one strip $2 \times 5\frac{1}{4}$ in / 5.1×13.3 cm. Cut

the same for section 10.

For section 8, cut one rectangle 5 × 16½ in / 12.7 × 41.9 cm.

For section 9, cut one rectangle 5½ × 17 in / 14 × 43.2 cm.

For section 10, cut one strip 1½ × 18¼ in / 3.8 × 46.4 cm.

4. From bright pink D, for section 1, bond and cut two small circles (Circle B) and one large circle (Circle D). Bond and cut four hearts (Heart A). Bond and cut the same motifs for section 13.

For section 2, cut one strip 2¼ × 3½ in / 5.7 × 8.9 cm.

For section 3, cut two squares 2 × 2 in / 5.1 × 5.1 cm, and two pieces 2 × 2¼ in / 5.1 × 5.7 cm.

For section 4, bond and cut one circle (Circle B), and one square 2 × 2 in / 5.1 × 5.1 cm.

For section 5, bond and cut two squares (Square A), one star (Star B), and one circle (Circle B).

For section 6, cut one rectangle 4½ × 5½ in / 11.4 × 14 cm. Bond and cut one strip ½ × 3 in / 1.3 × 7.6 cm. Bond and cut one set of lips.

For section 7, cut one rectangle 15½ × 17¾ in / 39.4 × 45.1 cm for the Sleeping Cat background.

For section 7a, bond and cut one circle (Circle C), and one star (Star E). Bond and cut one strip 1 × 2¾ in / 2.5 × 7 cm. Cut the same for section 10.

For section 8, cut one strip 1¾ × 12 in / 4.4 × 30.5 cm.

For section 9, cut one strip 1¾ × 7½ in / 4.4 × 19.1 cm.

For section 10, cut one strip 2 × 8 in / 5.1 × 20.3 cm.

For section 11, bond and cut one strip 1 × 2½ in / 2.5 × 6.4 cm. Cut one rectangular shape 4¼ × 5 in / 10.8 × 12.7 cm.

For section 12, bond and cut one circle (Circle D) and one square (Square C).

5. From the small floral scraps E, for section 3, cut three squares 2 × 2 in / 5.1 × 5.1 cm, and one piece 2 × 2¼ in / 5.1 × 5.7 cm.

6. From light blue F, for section 3, cut one piece 5½ × 6½ in / 14 × 16.5 cm.

For section 6, cut one rectangle 3½ × 5 in / 8.9 × 14 cm. Bond and cut one pupil for the eye.

For section 11, bond and cut one rectangle 2 × 2½ in / 5.1 × 6.4 cm.

For section 12, cut one rectangle 4 × 6 in / 10.2 × 15.2 cm.

7. From bright blue G, for section 1, bond and cut two circles (Circle D). Cut the same for section 13.

For section 2, cut six squares 2¼ × 2¼ in / 5.7 × 5.7 cm. Cut two rectangles 2¼ × 2⅝ in / 5.7 × 6.7 cm.

For section 7a, cut three rectangles 2¾ × 4 in / 7 × 10.2 cm (half will be used for section 10).

For section 10, cut one strip 2 × 8 in / 5.1 × 20.3 cm.

8. From dark blue H for section 4, cut one rectangle 4 × 4½ in / 10.2 × 11.4 cm.

For section 8a, cut one rectangle 5½ × 6½ in / 14 × 16.5 cm.

For section 10, cut one square 2 × 2 in / 5.1 × 5.1 cm.

For section 11, cut one rectangle 4 × 5 in / 10.2 × 12.7 cm.

9. From lavender I, for section 1, cut four squares 4¼ × 4¼ in / 10.8 × 10.8 cm. Cut the same for section 13.

For section 3, cut one piece 2 × 4 in / 5.1 × 10.2 cm.

For section 4, cut one rectangle 4 × 4½ in / 10.2 × 11.4 cm.

For section 5, bond and cut one square (Square A).

For section 7a, bond and cut one circle (Circle F). Cut the same for section 10.

For section 11, cut one rectangle 4¼ × 5 in / 10.8 × 12.7 cm.

10. From light purple J, for section 3, cut one piece 3 × 12½ in / 7.6 × 31.8 cm.

For section 5, cut one strip 2¾ × 9½ in / 7 × 24.1 cm.

Bond the remaining fabric.

For section 7a, cut one heart. Cut the same for section 10.

For section 12, cut one square (Square A) and one square (Square B).

11. From dark purple K, bond the reverse of the fabric and for section 1, cut two hearts (Heart A). Cut the same for section 13.

For section 5, cut one circle (Circle E).

For section 8, cut one strip ½ × 12 in / 1.3 × 30.5 cm.

For section 9, cut one strip ½ × 7½ in / 1.3 × 19.1 cm.

12. From plaid L, bond and cut the four cats.

13. From yellow and pink floral scraps M, bond and cut the initials of your choice.

14. From yellow N, for section 3, cut one square 2 × 2 in / 5.1 × 5.1 cm. Bond the remaining fabric.

For section 4, cut one circle (Circle A). Cut one strip 1 × 2 in / 2.5 × 5.1 cm.

For section 5, cut one circle (Circle C), and one circle (Circle E).

For section 6, cut one star (Star C).

For section 7a, cut one rectangle 2¾ × 3 in / 7 × 7.6 cm. Cut the same for section 10.

For section 8a, cut one starman.
For section 11, cut one strip 1 × 2½ in /
2.5 × 6.4 cm. Cut one star (Star A).
For section 12, cut one star (Star C).

15. From bright green O, bond the
reverse of the whole fabric and for
section 1 cut one circle (Circle A).
Cut the same for section 13.
For section 3, cut one whole fish.
For section 5, cut one strip ¾ × 2¼ in /
1.9 × 5.7 cm.
For section 7a, cut one strip ½ × 5 in /
1.3 × 12.7 cm, one strip ½ × 6½ in /
1.3 × 16.5 cm, one strip ½ × 7½ in / 1.3 ×
19.1 cm, one strip ½ × 9 in / 1.3 ×
22.9 cm, and one strip ½ × 11 in / 1.3 ×
28 cm. Cut ten leaves. Cut the same
for section 10.
For section 8, cut one strip ½ × 12 in /
1.3 × 30.5 cm.
For section 9, cut one strip ½ × 7½ in /
1.3 × 19 cm.
For section 12, bond and cut one fish
head and one fish tail.

16. From white P, for section 1, cut
one piece 2¼ × 4¼ in / 5.7 × 10.8 cm.
Cut the same for section 13.
For section 6, cut one rectangle 4½ ×
5½ in / 11.4 × 14 cm. Bond and cut one
eye.
For section 7a, cut two rectangles
15½ × 17¾ in / 39.4 × 45.1 cm.
For section 10, cut one rectangle
14½ × 17 in / 35.6 × 43.2 cm.

17. From black Q, for section 1, cut
eight strips 1¼ × 4¼ in / 3.1 × 10.8 cm.
Cut the same for section 13.
For section 4, bond and cut two strips
¼ × 2 in / 0.6 × 5.1 cm.
For section 5, bond and cut one
rectangle 2 × 2¼ in / 5.1 × 5.7 cm. Cut
one square (Square A).
For section 7a, cut five strips 1 × 4 in /
2.5 × 10.2 cm (half will be used for
section 10). Bond and cut one strip
½ × 2¾ in / 1.3 × 7 cm. Bond and cut
one circle (Circle C). Cut the same

This is the original design. Use the illustration on page 74 as your stitching guide.

for section 10.
For section 8, cut one square 4 × 4 in /
10.2 × 10.2 cm.
For section 9, cut one square 4 × 4 in /
10.2 × 10.2 cm. Bond and cut one pocket
flap liner. Bond and cut one shape of
the complete pocket and flap pattern.
For section 10, cut one strip 2 × 6 in /
5.1 × 15.2 cm.
For section 11, bond and cut two

strips ⅜ × 2½ in / 1 × 6.4 cm, and one
strip ½ × 2½ in / 1.3 × 6.4 cm.

18. For the white border, for the
right-hand side cut one length 3 × 48 in /
7.6 × 121.9 cm. For the left-hand side
cut one strip 3 × 56 in / 7.6 × 142.2 cm.
For the top cut one strip 3 × 47 in /
7.6 × 119.4 cm, cut the same for the
bottom border.

MAKING UP

■ Use a ¼ in / 0.6 cm seam allowance throughout. Pin and baste each step before stitching. Trim and tidy the seam allowances as you work. Press all seams towards the darkest color after each step. Refer to the black and white illustration as a guide to color placement. Read the General Techniques chapter for instructions on making continuous binding.

1. To make sections 1 and 13, use the black and white illustration as a guide to color placement, and bond and appliqué the hearts and circles to the appropriate squares. Sew the black 4¼ in / 10.8 cm lengths between the pink and lavender squares. Add the white rectangle to the right-hand side of each heart border. Put to one side.

2. To make section 2, stitch the blue and pink squares together in alternate colors, beginning and ending with a blue rectangle. Stitch a bright pink strip to the top.

3. To make section 3, bond, appliqué and embroider the whole fish to the blue rectangle. Stitch on a button for the eye. Stitch together the two 3½ in / 8.9 cm squares, and then stitch them to the top of the fish panel. Sew together the pink and lavender strips at one short end and sew these to the fish panel. Stitch together the 2 in / 5.1 cm squares into a block of nine. Stitch together the six remaining 2¼ in / 5.7 cm squares into a block of six – three blocks wide and two deep. Stitch the block of six to the bottom of the block of nine. Stitch this pieced block to the fish panel. Stitch the light purple strip to the bottom.

4. To make section 4, bond, appliqué and embroider the Proud Cat to the large rectangle. Stitch the pale pink

1¾ in / 4.5 cm strip to the light pink 10 in / 25.4 cm strip and sew both to the bottom of the cat panel. Bond and appliqué the hearts, circles and square motifs to the appropriate color blocks. Stitch the blocks together in the order shown, and stitch this pieced strip to the cat panel.

5. To make section 5, bond and appliqué the star, squares, strips and circles to the light pink rectangle. Stitch the light purple strip to the bottom of the appliquéd panel. Sew together sections 3, 4 and 5.

6. To make section 6, stitch the 14½ in / 39.4 cm strip to the bottom of the pale pink square. Bond and

appliqué the eye to the light pink rectangle. Embroider the details with back stitch using three strands of embroidery thread. Bond and appliqué the remaining motifs to the appropriate color blocks. Stitch the blocks together in the order shown, then stitch the pieced strip to the plain panel. Do not bond or appliqué the cat at this point.

7. To make section 7, bond and appliqué the Sleeping Cat to the bright pink rectangle, embroider the features and put to one side.

8. To make sections 7a and 10, stitch together alternate pink, blue, and black 4 in / 10.2 cm strips. Trim one long edge to make a strip 3½ in / 8.9 cm wide. Cut in half to make two strips 1¾ in / 4.4 cm wide.

9. Make both flower panels at the same time. Arrange each of the five ½ in / 1.3 cm wide bright green stems on the appropriate white rectangle. Position the leaves, heart, circles, squares, strips and star. Bond and appliqué in place. To make the flower flap hiding the Sleeping Cat, with right sides together, pin the flower flap to the second white rectangle and stitch around the sides and bottom. Turn right side out. Stitch buttonholes at each end of the bottom of the flap.

10. Stitch the alternate pink, black, blue, and black strip to the left-hand side of the flower flap for section 10, and to the right-hand side of the Sleeping Cat panel for section 7. Stitch section 6 and the Sleeping Cat panel together. Stitch these to sections 3, 4 and 5 above.

11. To stitch the flower flap over the Sleeping Cat panel, draw a light pencil line on the flower panel backing ¼ in /

0.6 cm from the top raw edge. With right sides facing, align the ruled pencil line with the seam joining the Sleeping Cat panel to sections 4 and 5. Stitch on the drawn pencil line, then fold back the flower panel over the stitched line. Topstitch ¼ in / 0.6 cm from the top edge. Stitch on the buttons to align with the buttonholes.

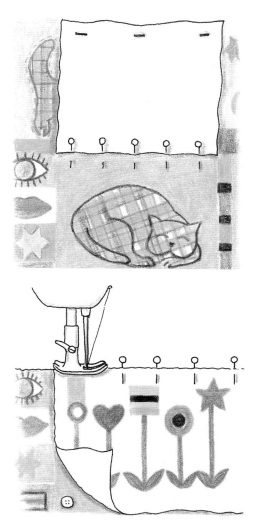

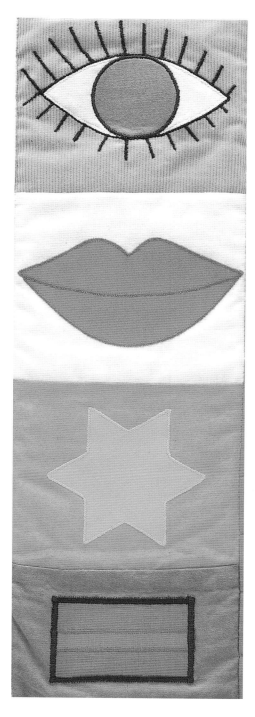

12. Bond and appliqué the Leaping Cat to sections 3 and 6. Embroider the details.

13. To make sections 8 and 9, rule a light pencil line 1⅝ in / 4.1 cm from the top of the medium pink rectangle for section 8, and 1⅞ in / 4.7 cm from the top of section 9, as a guide for bonding the center bright pink strip. Position the strip so that it meets the marked pencil line and is at the left-

hand side of the rectangle for section 8, and at the right-hand side for section 9. Bond in position. Place the purple and bright green strips at the top and bottom of the bright pink strip, so that they are slightly overlapping. Bond and appliqué.

14. Bond and appliqué your chosen initials on the black squares. Bond each square to either section 8 or 9.

15. To make the pocket at the right-hand side of the initial on section 9, bond the pocket flap lining to the wrong side of the pocket, aligning curved raw edges. Fold the stiff net in half and pin to the right side of the pocket. Bond fusible webbing to the reverse of the lower half of the pocket.

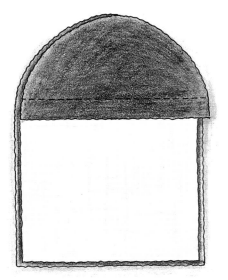

Make a buttonhole in the center of the flap. Bind the folded edge. Beginning at one corner of the pocket, bind the whole pocket. Turn under the raw edges of the tape and overlap the two ends. Stitch a button in place.

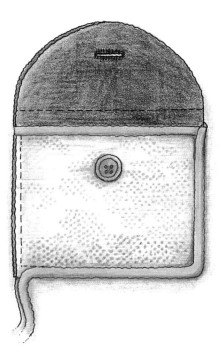

Bond the pocket shape to section 9 at the right-hand side of the initial. Stitch the pocket flap in place. Appliqué around the outer raw edges. Stitch sections 8 and 9 to the quilt, leaving a gap for the starman to be stitched in place. Stitch section 2 to the left-hand side of the quilt.

16. To make section 8a, the starman, bond and appliqué the ribbon to the arms of the starman. Bond and appliqué the starman to the dark blue rectangle. Embroider his face. Put to one side.

17. To complete section 10, stitch the medium pink strip to the top of the flower panel. To make the pieced border for the bottom, cut random lengths from the remaining 2 in / 5.1 cm wide strips and piece together a border 2 × 18¼ in / 5.1 × 46.4 cm. Stitch the border to the bottom of the panel.

18. To make section 11, using the black and white line illustrations as a guide to color placement, bond and appliqué the shapes to the appropriate 4½ in / 11.4 cm wide blocks. For the top block, bond the motif to the lower half of the block, so that the starman does not cover part of it. Stitch the blocks together in the order shown.

19. To make section 12, bond and appliqué the Satisfied Cat to the left-hand side of the plaid background. Bond and appliqué the circles, squares and star to the right-hand side of the cat. Bond and appliqué the fish to the light blue rectangle and embroider the details. Bond the light blue rectangle to the bottom right of the cat panel. Stitch together sections 10, 11 and 12, aligning the bottom raw edges.

20. Sew on the white cotton right-hand side border, trimming to fit where necessary, then sew sections 1 and 13 in position. Stitch on the white left-hand side border, then the top and bottom white borders.

21. To make the pieced outer border, gather together the brightest and darkest scraps used in the quilt and from these cut and piece strips 1¾ in / 4.4 cm wide and in varying lengths, sufficient to make up two borders 1¾ × 62 in / 4.4 × 157.5 cm for the left- and right-hand side, and two borders 1¾ × 54 in / 4.4 × 137.2 cm for the top and bottom borders.

22. Make up the quilt sandwich following the instructions on page 106.

23. Bind the quilt following the instructions for single-fold binding on page 109.

24. Sew bright buttons at random on top and embellish with yo-yos. To make each yo-yo using your circle templates, from fabric cut one circle 4½ in / 11.4 cm, and one circle 2½ in / 6.4 cm. Rough cut one circle 2½ in / 6.4 cm from fusible webbing and fuse to the reverse of the smaller circle. Trim to the exact size. Remove the paper backing and fuse the smaller circle to the center of the larger circle.

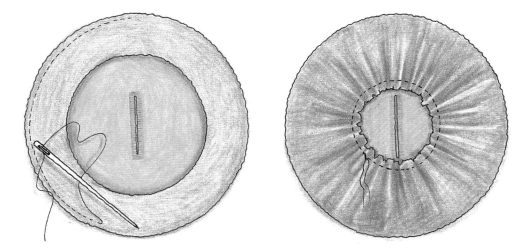

25. In the center make a buttonhole the required length, following the instructions on page 111. Turn under a ¼ in / 0.6 cm seam at the raw edge of the circle, and run small gathering stitches around the seam allowance. Pull up the gathering stitches and knot the end of the thread.

26. Quilt around each of the cats, ⅛ in / 0.3 cm from the appliqué line. Quilt around the flowers and stems in section 10. Quilt all seams in-the-ditch. Quilt along all long seams and around the inner edge of the binding.

HEARTS AND FLOWERS ROMAN BLIND

SIZE 42 × 50 in / 106.7 × 127 cm
adapt the measurements to your own requirements

DETERMINING THE REQUIRED YARDAGE FOR YOUR BLIND

1. Measure the width of your window and add to this measurement 4 in / 10.2 cm for seam allowances.

2. Measure the length of your window and add to this measurement 6 in / 15.2 cm for the hems.

MATERIALS

2 yd / 2 m of 60 in / 152 cm wide white cotton for the blind

2 yd / 2 m of 60 in / 152 cm wide white cotton for the lining

9 yd / 8.25 m bias tape 1 in / 2.5 cm wide to thread the wooden dowel through

Seven lengths of wooden dowel 42 in / 110 cm and ¼ in / 0.6 cm diameter

42 in / 110 cm of 2 × ½ in / 5 × 1.3 cm wooden batten to fasten to the top of the blind and the window frame

20 yd / 18.3 m of festoon blind cord

30 festoon rings

One small cleat

Five metal eyelets

Fabric paints in assorted colors for stencils

Stencil brushes

Card or stencil waxed cardboard to make stencils

Craft knife

Paper masking tape

1½ yd / 1.5 m Stick and Sew Velcro

Scrap paper

White paint for the wooden batten

CUTTING

■ Wash each fabric separately and press before cutting.

1. Cut the blind to the size of your measurements.

2. Cut the lining ½ in / 1.3 cm smaller than the width of your finished size and 6 in / 15.2 cm longer.

3. Trace the patterns provided to make templates for each of the stencils. Transfer the tracing into the center of a rectangular shape cardboard. Cut each shape out of cardboard using a sharp craft knife and without cutting into the border. The flower border is made up of nine flowers and stems and two half flowers and stems at each edge. You will need sufficient templates to randomly cover the top of the blind.

4. For the bias tape pockets to encase the wooden dowel, cut seven lengths each 42 in / 106.7 cm.

5. Cut the length of festoon cord into five equal pieces.

MAKING UP

■ When using fabric paints and stencils, use one color at a time and apply paint to each part of each motif that uses the same color. Always use a clean, dry brush and use a different brush for each color application. Dab the brush into the paint and shake off the excess on scrap paper. A second layer of color can always be applied if the first is not a strong enough shade, but it is practically impossible to lighten color if the original application is too dark. Never use water. Allow each color to dry before adding a neighboring color.

1. Protect your working area with a thick layer of scrap paper.

2. Check that the raw edges are cut at a perfect right angle to the selvages and trim accordingly, so that all raw edges are straight and even.

3. Turn under 2 in / 5.1 cm at each side of the blind and press. Turn under 3 in / 7.6 cm at the top and bottom and press. Open out the folded edges. Spread the fabric out right side up on the working surface with the long edges running away from you. Using masking tape secure the fabric around the edges to the paper, pulling the fabric taut.

4. Use the pressed foldline at each side of the blind as a guide. Do not breach this foldline with fabric paint. Draw a guideline across the width of the blind 4 in / 10.2 cm up from the bottom raw edge and stick masking tape across, so that the top edge of the tape meets the marked guideline. Measure and draw a second guideline 1 in / 2.5 cm away from the first, and stick masking tape across so that the bottom edge of the tape meets the guideline. Further divide the 1 in / 2.5 cm space into random sections ranging from ½–4 in / 1.3–10.2 cm.

5. From your second marked guideline measure and draw a third line 3 in / 7.6 cm away. Stick masking

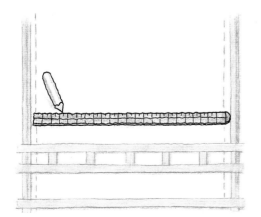

tape across the guideline, joining the top edge up to the pencil line. This third guideline is the point where the flower motifs begin. The stems on the blind we made are ½ in / 1.3 cm wide and are positioned 3⅞ in / 9.8 cm apart. From your third guideline mark with a fine pencil line the position of each of your stems. The smallest of the stems we made measures 5¼ in / 13.3 cm long, and the longest stem measures 9¼ in / 23.5 cm. Stick masking tape at a right angle to the third guideline joining up each side of each marked stem. Stick masking tape across the top of the stem to stop the fabric paint from bleeding.

6. Beginning with green paint, fill in each of the stems. Apply with a dabbing motion (not painting) filling in the ½ in / 1.3 cm space between the pieces of masking tape. Allow the paint to dry before removing the masking tape surround.

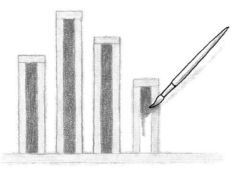

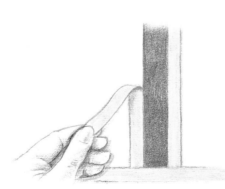

Using masking tape stick the leaf stencils to either side of the stem, and fill in with the paint. Fill in any green

in the random border at the bottom of the blind. Continue to build up each of the motifs, one color at a time, allowing each to dry before removing the stencil. Where a second color meets the first, stick masking tape across the end of the first, so that part of the fabric paint is covered with tape – it will not run or bleed provided you allow the first color to dry thoroughly before beginning with the second. When the stencilling is complete, remove the masking tape and following the manufacturer's instructions set the paint with a hot dry iron.

7. To prepare the bias tape pockets, turn under ¼ in / 0.6 cm on each raw edge and press. Put aside until step 9.

8. Center the lining on the blind with right sides facing. Pin and machine stitch the raw edges of the sides only to form a tubular shape. Overcast the raw edges. Turn right side out and press the blind, using the foldlines as your guide.

9. To make a hem at the bottom of the blind, turn under ½ in / 1.3 cm, and then turn under a further 2½ in / 6.4 cm to the wrong side, press. Open out the pressed foldlines. On the right side of the blind measure and mark

½ in / 1.3 cm below the second pressed foldline. Align one length of the prepared bias tape with the marked line, so that the left-hand edge meets the marked guideline.

10. Machine stitch in place along each long edge, leaving the short edges at the sides free to thread the dowel through. Fold the hem back into position and stitch in place using an invisible stitch. Turn under ½ in / 1.3 cm at the top of the blind and stitch the folded edges together.

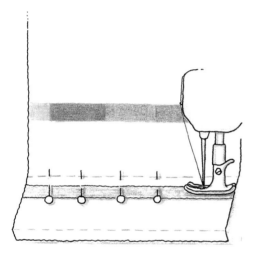

11. Along each side edge of the blind on the lining measure points 8 in / 20.3 cm apart. Pin and stitch 1 in / 2.5 cm wide bias tape pockets across every marked line, leaving the short edges free. Draw a guideline 3 in / 7.6 cm from the top of the lining and to this guideline sew the "stitch" side of the "Stick and Sew Velcro".

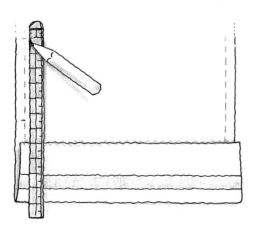

12. To mark the position of the festoon rings, on each strip of bias (except the hemline bias) mark a point close to each end. Mark the center point, then mark equal points between the edge and center marks on each strip.

13. Trim the dowel to the required length and thread one length through each bias pocket. Slipstitch the short ends of the bias to the lining using matching thread.

14. Stitch a festoon ring close to each end of the bias pocket and on each marked point.

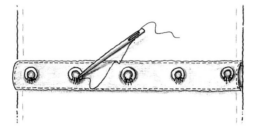

15. Working from the bottom of the blind upwards, thread each cord through each bottom ring and knot securely with a double knot. Continue threading each length of cord up through the vertical rows of rings. Put to one side.

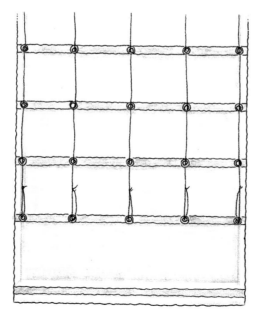

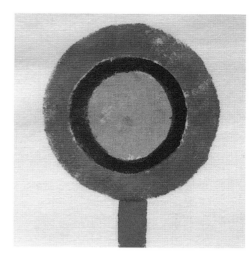

16. To prepare the wooden batten, although the batten will not be seen you may choose to paint it the same color as the blind. Measure and mark five points across the length of the batten. The points should align with the placement of the rings on the bias tape at the back of the blind. Screw metal eyelets into the marked points, close to one edge for the bottom of the batten. Thread the cords from the festoon rings through each of the metal eyelets, then thread each cord through the metal eyelets working left, so that all five cords, eventually thread through the metal eyelet on the far left of the blind.

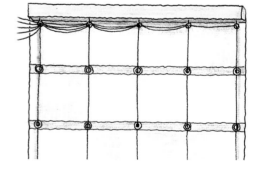

17. Stick Velcro to the top of the batten, so that it aligns with the Velcro on the blind. Fasten in position. Fasten the small cleat to the bottom left-hand side of the window frame. Braid the lengths of cord together and wrap around the cleat.

CANDY TABLELAMP

MATERIALS

■ Read the instructions to determine the required amount of bias binding for your lampshade.

Plain colored purchased lampshade

Bias binding

Bonded scraps for the motifs, pink, bright pink, lavenders, purple, blue, black, green, and yellow

6 × 12 in / 15 × 30 cm backing for the motifs, the same color as the lampshade or pale pink or white fabric

Heat resistant fabric glue/craft glue

CUTTING

■ Read page 106 for instructions on using fusible webbing.

1. Make templates for the motifs from the patterns provided for The Contented Cat Quilt. Bond the scrap fabric and rough cut sufficient of each motif to randomly scatter over the lampshade. Bond each motif to backing fabric and cut to the finished size. Smaller circles and squares can be bonded to the base motifs. Bond and cut ten to 15 tiny polka dots, ¼–⅜ in / 0.6–1 cm.

2. For the binding, measure the circumference of the top and bottom of the lampshade and add 2 in / 5.1 cm to each measurement. If you are using commercial pre-folded binding buy 1 in / 2.5 cm width. If you are making your own binding, cut strips 1¾ in / 4.5 cm wide × the required lengths and follow the instructions on page 109 for double-fold binding.

MAKING UP

■ Many adhesives work better if a small amount of adhesive is applied to the lampshade as well as to the wrong side of the motifs.

1. To bind the bottom of the lampshade, starting at the back and on the right side of the shade, align the lengthways center of the binding with the bottom edge of the lampshade and glue the top half of the binding to the edge of the lampshade, stretching slightly to fit.

2. Trim the binding so that there is a ¾ in / 1.9 cm overlap. Turn under ½ in / 1.3 cm on the overlapping raw edge and stick in place. Allow to dry.

3. Turn the binding under to the inside of the shade, glue in place following the manufacturer's instructions and allow to dry.

4. Repeat with the top edge. Where the binding crosses any part of the wire frame snip and trim the binding with the points of very sharp scissors.

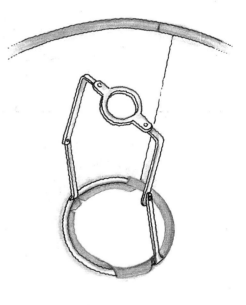

5. To decorate the lamp, trim the edges of each motif so that no backing shows. The bonding makes a stable raw edge and so no further finishing is necessary. However, if you choose, stitch very close satin stitch in bright colors around each raw edge. Glue the candy motifs to the shade following the manufacturer's instructions. Keep a damp cloth available to wipe away any excess glue that seeps out around the edges.

The
BOY'S
BEDROOM

For this room, I tried to imagine the colors and motifs that would appeal to a young boy's spirit of adventure. My storyboard was made up of colors from the great outdoors and harks back to log cabins and cowboys from frontier lands of pioneer days. I chose warm browns of the great red wood timbers, the shady greens of conifer forests and the rich reds of the wild cherry and crab apple trees. Added to this is a showy dash of bright blue and fiery red to complete the picture.

SQUIRREL QUILT

SIZE 42½ × 66 in / 108 × 167.6 cm

MATERIALS

■ All measurements are based on a fabric width of 45 in / 114.3 cm.

⅓ yd / 0.3 m fawn flower print flannel for the blocks

1 yd / 1 m red flannel for the blocks and outer border

⅓ yd / 0.3 m red spot flannel for two blocks

⅓ yd / 0.3 m plain fawn flannel for three blocks

⅔ yd / 0.6 m russet flannel for the inner border

9 in / 23 cm square green / blue flannel for the trees and two corners

2 yd / 1.8 m plain green flannel for backing, trees and corners

2 yd / 1.8 m of 4 oz / 100 gm polyester batting

½ yd / 0.5 m spotted fawn flannel for the squirrels

¾ yd / 0.7 m mid-brown flannel for the seminole patchwork

1 yd / 1 m navy print flannel for the seminole patchwork

1 yd / 1 m brown plaid flannel for tree stumps and binding

6½ yd / 6 m piping cord

Fabric marker pen

1 yd / 1 m fusible webbing

Embroidery floss for tying the quilt

CUTTING

■ Before cutting, dampen all wool and corduroy fabrics and iron dry to prevent shrinkage when washing. Cut all the largest pieces first from your fabric. Read the General Techniques chapter for instructions on making templates, using fusible webbing, covering piping cord, and appliqué.

1. For the quilt top, cut six plain red squares, two red spot squares, three fawn squares and four fawn patterned squares, each 9½ in / 24.1 cm.

2. From spotted fawn cut six left facing squirrels and acorns and two

right facing squirrels and acorns. From the green / blue and green flannel cut seven trees alternating the stripes of color. Cut seven tree stumps from one end of the tartan fabric. Rough cut the same shapes from fusible webbing. Bond fusible webbing to the reverse of the fabric shapes, then trim the paper to the same size as the fabric shape.

3. For the seminole patchwork sashing strips, across the width of the fabric cut lengths of mid-brown 2 in / 5.1 cm wide and sufficient to make up 7½ yd / 7 m. From the navy print, cut 2 in / 5.1 cm wide strips sufficient to make up two lengths 7½ yd / 7 m long. Cut 1 in / 2.5 cm strips sufficient to make up two lengths 7½ yd / 7 m long from the remaining navy print.

4. For the pieced center squares, from fabric scraps cut eight center squares 2 in / 5.1 cm, eight squares 2¾ in / 7 cm, and eight squares 3½ in / 8.9 cm. Cut the 2¾ in / 7 cm squares across the diagonal to make two triangles, and again across the diagonal to make four triangles. Repeat with the 3½ in / 8.9 cm squares.

5. For the russet border, cut six strips 3½ × 45 in / 8.9 × 114.3 cm.

6. For the red outer border, cut six strips 45 × 2½ in / 114.3 × 6.4 cm

7. For each of the four Churn Dash corners, cut five 1½ in / 3.8 cm squares from one color and four 1½ in / 3.8 cm squares from a second color. Cut two of each color in half across the diagonal to make eight triangles, and two of each color in half across the length to make eight rectangles.

MAKING UP

■ Use a ¼ in / 0.6 cm seam allowance throughout. Pin and baste each step before stitching. Trim and tidy the seam allowances as you work. Press all seams towards the darkest color after each step.

1. To make the appliqué blocks, bond each squirrel and acorn to the appropriate color background. Bond each striped tree and tree stump to a background square. Satin stitch around the outline and each raw edge.

2. To make the seminole patchwork sashing, stitch each of the 2 in / 5.1 cm wide lengths together to form the requisite 7½ yd / 7 m lengths. With right sides together stitch the mid-brown length between the two navy 2 in / 5.1 cm strips.

3. From the 7½ yd / 7 m length cut 2 in / 5.1 cm strips each made up of three fabrics.

4. Re-assemble and stitch the strips in a staggered configuration. Look at the illustration below to work out and understand which seams should align when stitching the strips together.

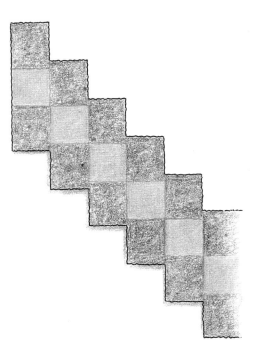

5. Using a light pencil draw a line ¼ in / 0.6 cm from the points of the brown squares. Trim the excess fabric.

6. To each side of the block, stitch the remaining 7½ yd / 7 m lengths, then cut 22 strips of sashing each

9½ in / 24.1 cm long. Each strip of seminole sashing should have four whole brown squares and two half-triangle squares.

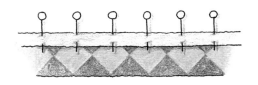

7. To make the pieced center squares which join the sashing blocks together, turn under and press ¼ in / 0.6 cm seam on all sides of the squares and triangles as a stitching line guide. Stitch one small triangle to each edge of each square to make a square 2¼ in / 5.7 cm. Repeat stitching the larger triangles to each side of the squares.

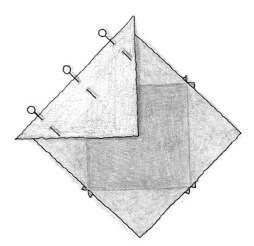

8. To make up the top row of the center panel, stitch one seminole sashing strip to the right side of one squirrel block. Add a tree block to the other side of the strip. To this stitch a second floating square sashing strip. Finish with a second squirrel block. Continue to make up five panels of three blocks in this way.

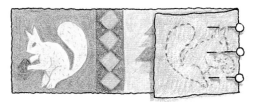

9. To make the joining strips, stitch a pieced center square between two sashing strips. Add a second center square and a third sashing strip to one side. Repeat to make four lengths. Stitch one length between two squirrel and tree panels.

10. To make each of the four Churn Dash blocks, stitch alternate color triangles together across the diagonal to make four squares.

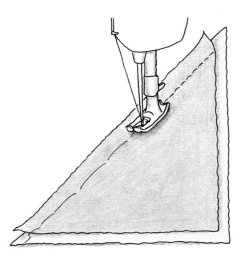

Stitch alternate color rectangles together to make four squares. Stitch together into two rows of half-triangle square, half-rectangle square, half triangle square for the top and bottom, and half rectangle square, square, half rectangle square for the middle. Stitch the three rows into a block.

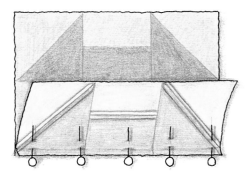

11. To make the russet border, stitch two 3½ in / 8.9 cm wide lengths together. Center the join on the side of the panel and trim the ends to the

length of your pieced quilt top. Repeat with two further strips. Trim the remaining two strips to the width of your pieced quilt top.

12. Stitch the side borders to each side of the quilt.

13. Stitch one Churn Dash block to each end of the top and bottom russet borders. Stitch the borders to the quilt.

14. To make the red outer border, stitch together two lengths of fabric for each side of the quilt. Find the seam in the middle of the russet border and match with the middle of the border and pin the two together with right sides facing. Stitch in position and trim the ends. Stitch the top and bottom borders to each end.

15. For instructions on making the quilt sandwich follow the instructions on page 106. To finish, the quilt is tied at the corner of every squirrel block and every tree block. Follow the instructions on page 107.

16. To make continuous binding 6½ yd / 6.1 m long and 2 in / 5.1 cm wide to cover the piping cord, use the plaid and follow the instructions in the General Techniques chapter on page 108. Stitch to the quilt front following the instructions on page 96.

COWBOY BOLSTER CUSHION

SIZE 19¾ × 11 × 11 in / 50.2 × 28 × 28 cm

MATERIALS

- All measurements are based on a fabric width of 45 in / 114.3 cm.
- ½ yd / 0.5 m brown flannel or wool
- ¾ yd / 0.7 m fawn flannel or wool
- 2 yd / 2 m cotton lining
- Scraps for appliqué motifs
- 18 × 22 in / 46 × 56 cm green corduroy for piping and trees
- ½ yd / 0.5 m fusible webbing
- ½ yd / 0.5 m tearaway stabilizer
- 2¼ yd / 2.1 m of No 3 piping cord
- One 18 in / 46 cm zipper

CUTTING

■ Before cutting, dampen all wool and corduroy fabrics and iron dry to prevent shrinkage when washing. Read the General Techniques chapter for instructions on using fusible webbing, making templates and appliqué.

1. For lining, cut one piece 37 × 21 in / 94 × 53.3 cm. Cut two circles 11¾ in / 29.8 cm diameter for the sides.

2. For the cushion, cut two lengths of brown, and three lengths of fawn 9½ × 24 in / 24.1 × 61 cm. From the fawn cut two circles 11¾ in / 29.8 cm diameter for the sides.

3. Cut each motif from fabric scraps and roughly from fusible webbing. Bond fusible webbing to the reverse of each shape, then trim to the exact size.

MAKING UP

■ Use a ¼ in / 0.6 cm seam allowance throughout. Pin and baste each step before stitching. Bond all fabrics wrong side to right side. Trim and tidy the seam allowances as you work. Press all seams towards the darkest color after each step.

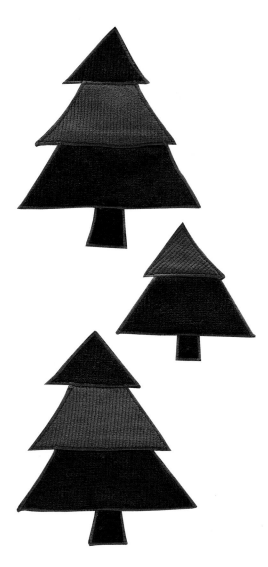

1. To make the panel, place the cotton lining right side down on a clean, flat surface. On top, in the center, and at an angle, place a fawn length right side up. Place a brown length on top, with right sides facing.

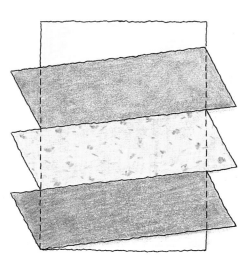

Machine stitch the two together at the top edge to the backing. Machine stitch alternate fawn and brown strips above and below these two. Trim the pieced panel to make a rectangle 20½ × 38 in / 52.1 × 96.5 cm.

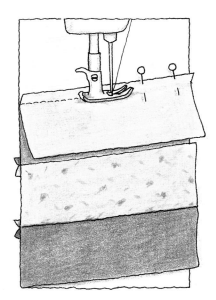

2. Position the motifs on the background. Bond and appliqué the cowboy and horse and two or three trees to each brown and fawn strip. Turn under a ½ in / 1.3 cm seam at the top and bottom of the appliqué panel.

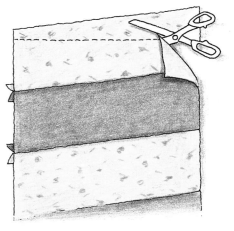

3. To make the circular ends, pin each lining to each fawn circle. Place tearaway stabilizer behind each to stop puckers when stitching. Bond and appliqué one large tree to each end, avoiding the pins. Remove the pins and tear away the excess stabilizer.

4. To insert the zip, position the cushion panel right side up on a clean, flat surface. At the bottom of the cushion, place the zip, right side down and with the opening to the left. Using a zipper foot, machine stitch one side of the zip to the cushion panel, taking care not to catch the teeth of the zip. Align the second half of the zip with the other end of the panel and machine stitch in place. Turn right side out. Stitch across the top and base of the zip and tab to reinforce the stitching.

5. To make 2¼ yd / 2.06 m of continuous binding 1½ in / 3.8 cm wide for the piping cord, use the 18 × 22 in / 45.7 × 55.9 cm green corduroy, and follow the instructions in the General Techniques chapter on page 108.

6. To cover the piping cord read the instructions on page 111. Cut the length of cord in two, half for each end of the cushion.

7. Starting directly below the center of the tree trunk, on the right side of the fabric, pin the piping around the edge of each circle, so that the cord overlaps by 1½ in / 3.8 cm and the raw edges align.

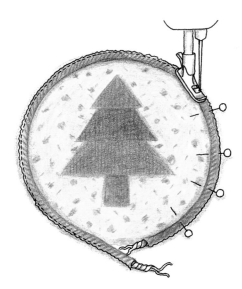

Cut and discard any excess cord. Undo the strands of the cord at each end, and twist the two ends together.

8. Overlap one side of the binding over the other and wrap tightly around the cord. Turn in ¼ in / 0.6 cm at the short ends. Pin and stitch.

9. To make up the cushion, turn the tube inside out. Fit one circular side to one end and stitch in place using the zipper foot on your sewing machine. Reinforce the stitching where the binding overlaps. Repeat this step stitching the second side to the other end of the cushion and leaving the zipper open to turn right side out.

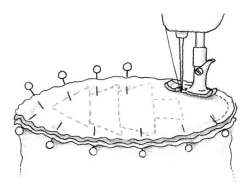

COUNTRY COWBOY RUG

SIZE 36 × 31½ in / 91.4 × 80 cm at the widest points

MATERIALS

■ All measurements are based on a fabric width of 45 in / 114.3 cm.

Four 18 in / 46 cm squares of brown washable felt for the background

1 yd / 1 m cotton backing

1 yd / 1 m pelmet-weight interfacing

1 yd / 1 m of 2 oz / 50 gm polyester batting

18 × 22 in / 46 × 56 cm red flannel for the trousers

18 × 22 in / 46 × 56 cm blue corduroy for the horse and waistcoat

18 × 22 in / 46 × 56 cm red check flannel for the shirt

18 × 22 in / 46 × 56 cm emerald green corduroy for the trees

18 × 22 in / 46 × 56 cm wine red for hat, neckerchief and roof

12 in / 30 cm square beige for face and hands

12 in / 30 cm square mid-brown for the boots

Fabric scraps for the remaining appliqué motifs

1¼ yd / 1.15 m fusible webbing

1 yd / 1 m tearaway stabilizer

4 yd / 3.7 m of 2 in / 5 cm wide red bias binding

2 yd / 1.85 m of 1 in / 2.5 cm wide red bias binding

Embroidery thread for the features

CUTTING

■ Before cutting, dampen all wool and corduroy fabrics and iron dry to prevent shrinkage when washing. Read the General Techniques chapter for instructions on making templates, enlarging a grid pattern, using fusible webbing and appliqué.

1. Make templates from the patterns provided. For the appliqué motifs, bond fusible webbing to the reverse of each fabric except the felt rug front. Place the templates right side down on the paper side of the webbing and the wrong side of the fabric, mark an

outline and cut the required number of each appliqué shape.

2. Make up a template for the rug. Work on a piece of paper the size of the finished rug. From side to side, at its widest point the rug measures 36 in / 91.4 cm. From center top to bottom it measures 31½ in / 80 cm.

MAKING UP

■ Use a ¼ in / 0.6 cm seam allowance throughout. Pin and baste each step before stitching. Stitch fabrics together with right sides facing unless stated otherwise. Trim and tidy the seam allowances as you work. Press all seams out after each step.

1. To make the background, stitch together the four pieces of brown felt to make one large square. Use your template to cut the rug shape.

2. Position the appliqué motifs on the rug front. When you are satisfied with the arrangement remove the paper backing and bond each to the background fabric, leaving the right hand and left fingertips until the lasso is in position.

3. To make the lasso held by the cowboy, turn under a ¼ in / 0.6 cm seam along each long edge of the 1 in / 2.5 cm red bias binding. Cut one 6 in / 15.2 cm length and turn under the corners at one end to make a point. Pin to the rug so that it runs parallel with the top of the cowboy's right leg. Pin and stitch the remaining length to the rug in a curved shape to resemble the end of the lasso rope. The 'rope' should end at the center top raw edge of the rug. Now bond the right hand and left fingertips in place.

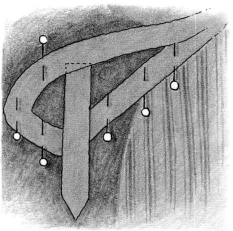

4. Pin the sheet of tearaway stabilizer behind the rug to stop any puckers appearing when stitching. Satin stitch the raw edges of the appliqué shapes in appropriate colors. Embroider the facial features using stem stitch. Tear away the stabilizer. Stitch on the lasso rope, easing in any necessary pleats.

5. To make up the rug, spread the backing fabric out on a clean, flat surface and smooth away any wrinkles. On top place the Vilene, batting and then the rug top. Baste all three layers together horizontally, vertically, diagonally and around the edge. Cut the batting, Vilene and backing to the same shape as the rug front.

6. Machine stitch through all four layers around the edge.

7. To bind the rug edges using the 2 in / 5.1 cm binding, turn under and press a small seam allowance along each edge of the binding. Fold the binding in half lengthways and press. Open out the binding. Pin one side of the binding to the rug front aligning the raw edges. Stitch in place. When stitching around the curved edges, clip into the seam allowance to help the binding lie flat and to stop puckers appearing. Overlap the start and finish points.

8. Fold the binding over the stitching line, the Vilene and batting to the back of the rug. Turn under ¼ in / 0.6 cm at the raw edge and slipstitch in place. Pull the binding taut so that any wrinkles are smoothed out.

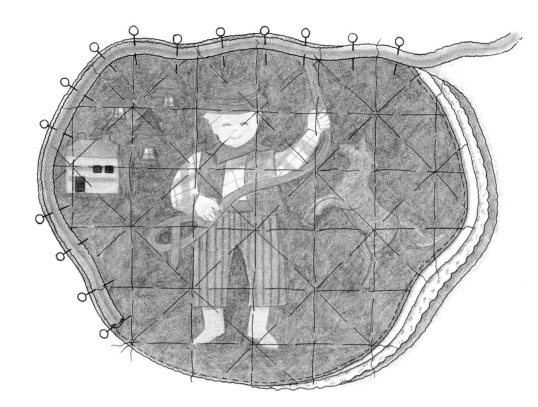

WOODLANDS TOYBOX COVER

SIZE $34 \times 18 \times 18$ in / $86.4 \times 45.7 \times 45.7$ cm
adapt the fabric requirements and measurements to fit your own box

MATERIALS

■ All measurements are based on a fabric width of 45 in / 114.3 cm.

¾ yd / 0.7 m red corduroy for the lid

1½ yd / 1.4 m brown for the sides

18×22 in / 46×56 cm blue for the horse

½ yd / 0.5 m green for the squares and trees

18×22 in / 46×56 cm blue flannel for the squares and trees

Fabric scraps for the remainder of the appliqué motifs

Small buttons for eyes

1 yd / 1 m tearaway stabilizer

1½ yd / 1.4 m fusible webbing

½ yd / 0.5 m pelmet-weight interfacing for the lid

½ yd / 0.5 m cotton backing for the lid

2 yd / 1.8 m Stick and Sew Velcro

CUTTING

■ Before cutting, dampen all wool and corduroy fabrics and iron dry to prevent shrinkage when washing. Read the General Techniques chapter for instructions on making templates, using fusible webbing and appliqué.

1. For the lid, cut the red corduroy $35¼ \times 19¼$ in / 89.5×48.9 cm, or $1¼$ in / 3.1 cm larger than the lid measurement. Cut the interfacing and backing to the same size.

2. For the sides, front and back, measure the circumference of your toybox and cut the fabric $1¼$ in / 3.1 cm larger all around.

3. For the appliqué shapes bond fusible webbing to the reverse of each remaining color. Place the templates right side down on the paper backing and mark an outline. Cut each shape.

4. From the blue flannel and remaining green flannel, cut sufficient squares $1½ \times 1½$ in / 3.8×3.8 cm for the border pattern.

5. From the Velcro cut small tabs for each corner of the lid. Use the remainder for sides, back and front.

MAKING UP

■ Use a ⅝ in / 1.6 cm seam allowance throughout. Pin and baste each step before stitching. Trim and tidy the seam allowances as you work. Press all seams towards the darkest color after each step.

1. To decorate the box lid, position each green and blue flannel 1½ in / 3.8 cm square on point on the border of the box lid, and bond in place. Place tearaway stabilizer under the red corduroy to stop puckers appearing when stitching, and pin to hold. Appliqué around each raw edge. Bond and machine appliqué each motif in place. Tear away the stabilizer. Stitch on the eyes and details.

2. On the right side of the backing fabric, for the lid, stitch tabs of Velcro to each corner ⅝ in / 1.6 cm from the outer edges.

3. Place the pelmet-weight interfacing on a clean, flat surface. On top place the lining right side up, then the corduroy lid right side down. Stitch the layers together using a ⅝ in / 1.6 cm seam allowance and leaving a large opening for turning.

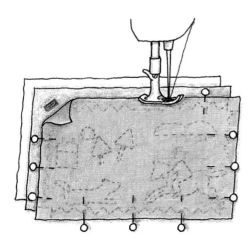

Turn the cover right side out, slipstitch across the opening and press the seam open.

4. To attach the lid to your toybox, stick the second side of the Velcro to the toybox, aligning the lengths with those on the lid.

5. To make the sides, front and back, turn under and press a ⅝ in / 1.6 cm seam at the bottom of the toybox piece. Baste long running stitches to mark the sides, back and front.

6. Bond and machine appliqué each motif in position following the instructions in step 1. Stitch on the eyes.

7. Stitch the two short ends together. The shape should fit snugly over your toybox. Adjust the seam accordingly.

8. Turn under ⅝ in / 1.6 cm seam at the top and bottom. Cover the raw edge of the top only with lengths of Velcro. Stitch the Velcro in place.

9. To attach the cover to the toybox, stick the remaining half of the Velcro to the toybox so that it aligns with the Velcro on the cover.

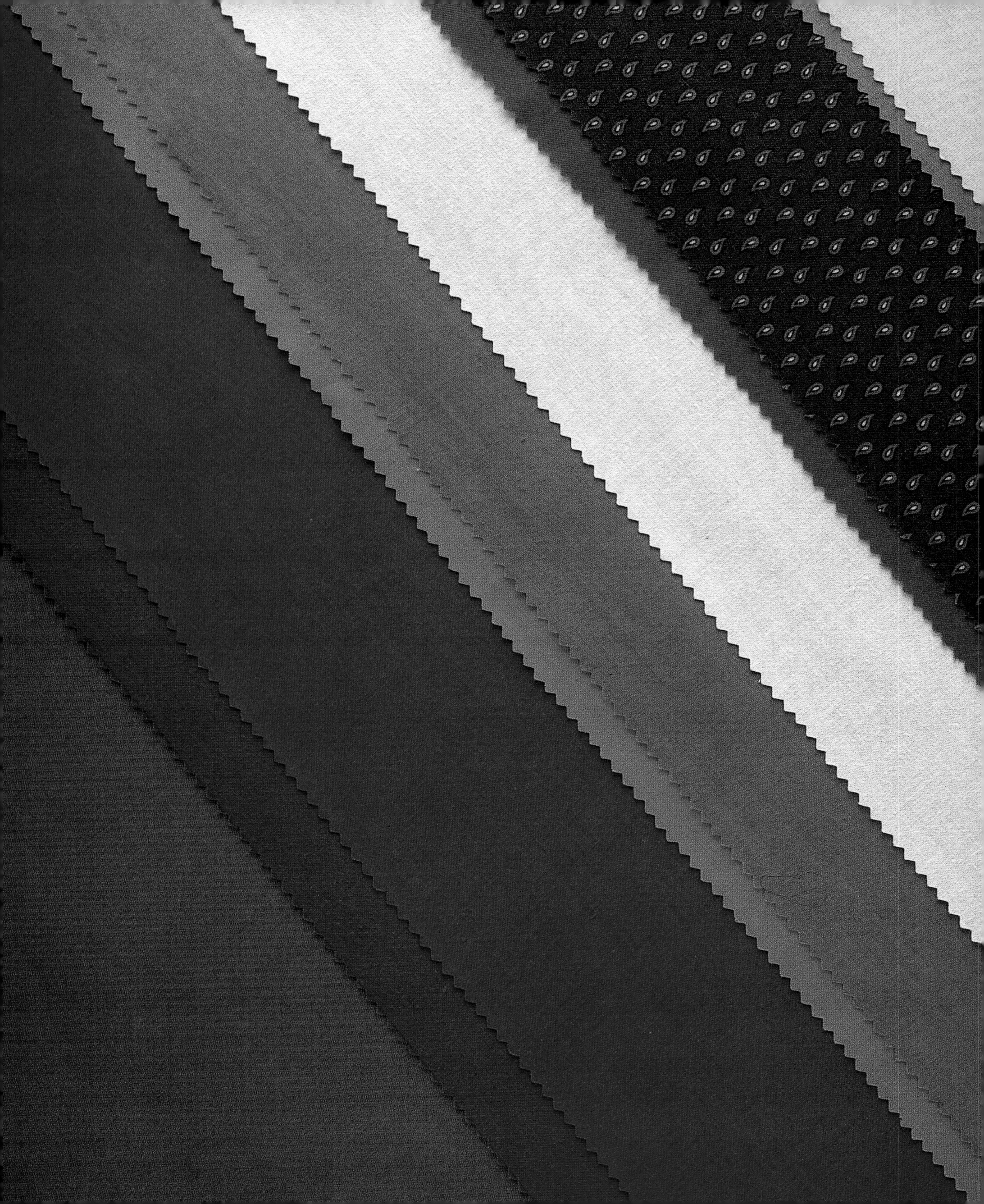

GENERAL TECHNIQUES

FABRICS

Each of the projects contained in this book has been made using a range of natural fabrics – felts, flannels, wools and cottons – all ideal for soft furnishings in the home. Felt and flannel textiles have recently re-emerged as popular decorating fabrics and in response, manufacturers have brought out exciting new ranges of colors with the decorator in mind. The ability of wool to take dye as a pure color has long made it a favorite with home decorators.

When choosing fabric for your projects it is wise to familiarize yourself with the different fabric types, properties, washing and after-care requirements, so that you can choose your fabric according to its intended use.

Cottons are the most practical and versatile of fabrics since they are hard wearing, colorfast, wash well, hold a crease, are generally easy to look after and relatively inexpensive.

A number of our projects are made of corduroy, a durable fabric, ideal for projects which will receive much wear and tear around the home. Corduroy has lengthways piles of cord which

have a smooth sheen finish but no give. This nap appears darker when looked at from one direction compared to the other. It is a characteristic which can be used to great advantage in many projects, providing a subtle but definite variation in color. The cross-grain of corduroy has more give than you may expect, making it ideal to use as binding, to ease around corners and gentle curves. Corduroy is available in fine needlecord or wider elephant cord weights.

Cotton flannel, normally associated with sheeting and children's night-wear was used exclusively in the squirrel quilt in the boy's bedroom. Flannel is a light-weight cotton, brushed on one side to give it a warm and soft appearance.

Felt is a non-woven, bonded fabric. Short fibers are matted and fused together with steam, soap and pummelling. Washing a wool jumper on a boil wash follows the same principle. Since felted fabrics, (including interfacing) have no warp and weft they are extremely easy to cut and sew with, making an ideal choice for appliqué work. When buying felt for projects that will be washed, always consult the label and

buy only washable felt. This is widely available in ready-cut 18 in / 46 cm squares or by the yard in limited colors. Other types of felt are liable to shrink, distort and change texture when washed.

Wool fabrics are knitted or woven. Only woven wool fabrics are used in projects in this book. Wool flannel is warm, does not crease as cotton creases and is easy to work with. However wool is a relatively weak fiber and shrinks when wet, so should be washed and ironed before it is cut. Projects using all-wool fabrics can safely be dry cleaned.

Most fabrics can be washed on a very cool setting, but it is advisable to follow manufacturer's instructions and test a small piece of fabric first.

- If you are using a variety of fabric types in your project, pick the same weight of fabric throughout.
- Wash each fabric before cutting to allow for shrinkage and to ensure your fabrics are colorfast.
- Pick thread a shade darker than the darkest color you are working with. Lay one single thread rather than the whole reel across the fabric to check the color match.

MAKING TEMPLATES

To make your own templates from each of the patterns provided you will need tracing paper, a pencil, thin cardboard and glue. First determine which of the pattern pieces need to be enlarged to the correct size. A good quality photocopying shop will increase the size of each of the templates for you.

Where motifs are made up of lots of shapes, in the cowboys for example, look carefully at each shape to see where it overlaps another shape or where it is itself overlapped. At the points where one shape is overlapped by another, an allowance of extra fabric has been made so that no gaps show through in the sewing.

Using a sheet of tracing paper and a pencil, trace each of the pieces. Stick your tracing to thin cardboard, then accurately cut around each shape.

To trace the design details of the flowers on the projects in The Garden Room onto the fabric, trace the complete flower motif onto a sheet of tracing paper. Place the tracing pencil marking side down, aligning it with the shape of the flower motif. Carefully draw over the pencil lines that you can see through the tracing paper and the image will appear on the fabric.

Remember to reverse each motif where necessary, since some shapes appear in more than one project.

ENLARGING A GRID

For the Butterfly Wallhanging and the Vine and Ivy Leaf Tablecloth in The Garden Room, the Country Cowboy Rug in The Boy's Bedroom, the cats for The Contented Cat Quilt in The Girl's Bedroom, and the Art Deco Wallhanging and Clarice Cliff Curtains in the Dining Room, you will need to make templates by enlarging the grid provided. Work on the principle that each square on the pattern represents one square inch or two and a half centimetres. To enlarge each grid you will need a large sheet of paper the finished size of the project on which to draw your

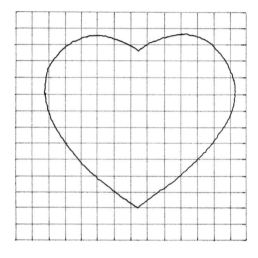

template, or buy 1 in / 2.5 cm 'dot and cross' paper which has a grid ready marked out. For the Vine and Ivy Leaf Tablecloth make up a sheet quarter of the size of the finished project. Accurately draw a grid of 1 in / 2.5 cm squares to cover the entire sheet of paper. To transfer the pattern to your grid, look at the pattern to see where the outline crosses the lines of the grid and plot these points on your 1 in / 2.5 cm grid. Continue plotting points on every line that the outline crosses. Once you are sure that all your points will meet up join up the dots to make the outline. Once you are satisfied with the shape, make templates for each individual piece following the instructions for Making Templates above. Do not cut up the pattern on the grid, use it as a reference guide for placing each of the motifs.

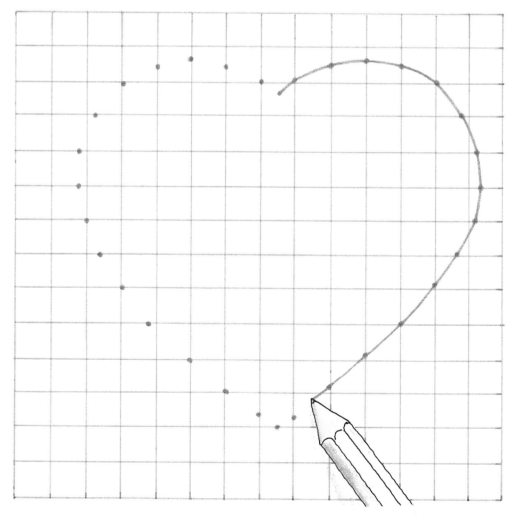

APPLIQUÉ USING FUSIBLE WEBBING

Fusible webbing provides a quick and convenient way of applying one fabric to another. It has one slightly rough side, the "web", and one smooth paper side. If the web sticks to either your iron or ironing board it is extremely difficult to remove. As a precaution, use baking parchment underneath your work to protect the ironing board, and on top of the fabric being bonded to protect your iron.

Draw or trace your pattern on the paper side of the fusible webbing. Remember to reverse your pattern pieces where necessary. If you have a large number of patterns or motifs to bond, trace them all onto the paper backing at the same time. Cut around each shape leaving a ¼ in / 0.6 cm margin. This will ensure the adhesive is carried right to the raw edge of your motif.

Place the fusible webbing, rough side down onto the wrong side of your fabric. Place baking parchment on top. Using a hot iron on the "wool" setting, bond the adhesive web to the fabric for ten seconds. Cut out each motif on your drawn pencil line. To apply the motif to the quilt top, remove the paper backing from the motif and bond in place as before.

Fusible webbing can be washed and dry cleaned.

Once bonded to the base fabrics, each of the shapes is stitched in place by machine. Satin stitch or zigzag stitches are used in varying widths depending on the project being stitched. For small appliqué pieces try setting your sewing machine to a stitch width of 2 and a stitch length of ½. For larger areas try a stitch width of 4. Most of the projects with the exception of The Dining Room are stitched using threads of the same color as the base fabric and changing colors where necessary. Pick a shade that looks slightly darker, this will emphasize the motifs and gives a strong, bold edge to your work. When working satin stitch begin with the machine foot on one raw edge of your motif, and the shape to the left or the right. The line of stitching should encase the raw edge, with half of the width of the stitch on the motif and half on the background fabric. If you are a novice try stitching with different stitch widths first on a fabric sample, then try easing the machine foot around curves and turning corners.

LAYERING A QUILT

Prepare a clean, flat surface – for some of the larger projects you may need to work with the floor as your surface. Spread the backing fabric out right side down and smooth out any wrinkles. On top center the batting, then the quilt top right side up. Pin the layers together, then baste horizontally, vertically, diagonally, and around each raw edge using long, straight, running stitches. Work from the center out and make your stitches about 1½ in / 3.8 cm long.

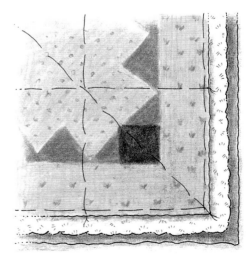

HAND QUILTING

Quilting holds the layers of the quilt or fabric together. It also has a decorative appeal since quilting can be used to add texture to a quilt; the rows of stitching add depth and visual interest. Hand quilting is worked using small running stitches usually ⅛ in / 0.3 cm long. However, to begin with, the length of the stitch is not so important as the evenness of the stitch. Thread your needle and knot the end of the thread. Begin in the center of the design and work outwards so that no puckers and wrinkles appear. Hold your needle at the front of the quilt, at the point close to where the first stitch will be made. Insert the needle through the front and the batting only, bringing it out at the point where the first stitch will be made. Give a sharp tug on the needle and the knot will pull through the quilt top and remain inside the batting. Experienced stitchers will pick up three to four stitches on their

needle in any one go, weaving the needle in and out of the fabric with a rocking motion.

TYING

Tying can be used to hold the quilt layers together or for decorative purposes. On the Squirrel Quilt in The Boy's Bedroom two strands of thick thread are used to tie the quilt at the corners and in the center seams of each of the blocks. Any type of fine wool or embroidery floss, even ribbon can be used to decorate a quilt. However the design will benefit if the type of thread and the tying is consistent all over the quilt top.

Thread a needle, but do not knot the end. Hold the needle perpendicular to the quilt top and at the point where you want the knot to appear. Stab through the layers of the quilt and pull the needle out at the back without letting the end of the thread disappear into the quilt surface. Leave 3–4 in / 7–10 cm at the front for tying. Take a small stitch ⅛ in / 0.3 cm long and bring the needle back up through the quilt top. Take the needle back down at the point where you made the first stitch. Pull tight to create a small stitch. Bring the needle up to the front once more at the point where the second stitch was made. Tie a square knot, first right over left, then left over right.

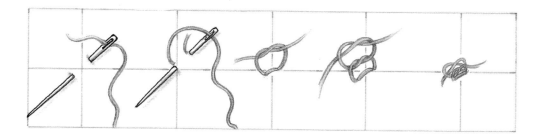

time folding the short end down to align with the bottom raw edge.

On the wrong side of the fabric draw lines parallel with the diagonal edge of the fabric and the width stated in your project instructions. Each line should run at an exact 45° angle. At the top left-hand corner of the fabric, mark the point 'A' with a pin. At the bottom left-hand side of the fabric, on the first ruled line, mark the point 'B' with a pin. Fold the fabric in half lengthways, right sides together. Align the top raw edges, then pull slightly on one half so that the marked pin points are aligned and each ruled line corresponds with a ruled line on the other half. Stitch the two sides together using ¼ in / 0.6 cm seam. Begin cutting around the spiral shape at the point where A and B meet. The spiral should unravel into one continuous length of binding. Press each diagonal seam outwards.

SELF-BINDING

In this method of binding, the backing wraps around the batting and the raw edge of the quilt top. Self-binding is the easiest and most economical way to bind a quilt. If you choose the backing as your binding be sure that the quality, color and pattern complement the quilt top.

Trim the quilt front and batting to the finished size of the quilt. Pin and baste the quilt horizontally, vertically, diagonally, and around each edge. Trim the backing 1 in / 2.5 cm larger all around. Turn under and press ¼ in / 0.6 cm around the raw edges of the backing.

Fold the corners in, fingerpress and trim the excess. Bring the excess fabric over to the front of the quilt, pin and baste in place. Slipstitch the folded edge in position.

CONTINUOUS BINDING

Used for quilts which have a curved edge such as the Country Cowboy Rug, where lengths of fabric must be cut on the cross grain. Spread out a large rectangle of fabric right side down on a flat surface. The rectangle should have square corners exact to the grain. To find the 45° angle or the true bias, pick up one corner, folding it across the rectangle so that the short vertical edge aligns with the top raw edge.

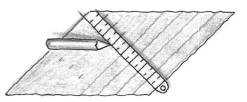

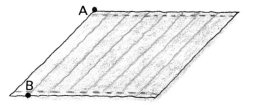

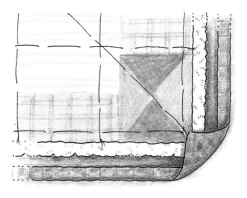

Finger crease, then cut the diagonal line. Repeat at the opposite side, this

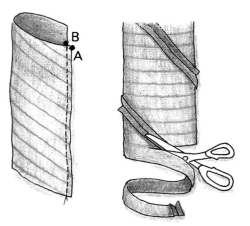

SINGLE-FOLD BINDING

For binding with a single-fold edge, strips are cut twice the desired width plus ½ in / 1.3 cm for seam allowances, and sufficiently long to equal the perimeter of the quilt plus 12 in / 30.5 cm for corner miters. On each long edge, turn under an exact ¼ in / 0.6 cm seam to the wrong side to hide the raw edges and press. Then fold the binding in half lengthways wrong sides together and press. The pressed center line forms the outer edge of the item to be bound.

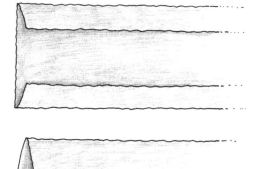

To attach the binding, open out the binding and align one lengthways raw edge with the raw edge of the project. Do not start at a corner. Pin and baste in position. Beginning 1½ in / 3.8 cm from the short end of the binding, machine straight stitch on the first foldline, and miter the corners following the instructions given.

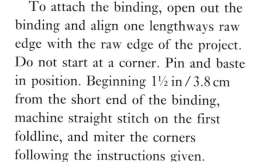

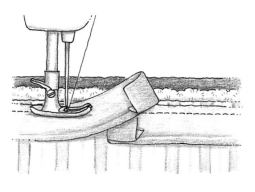

As you approach the end of the binding, stop stitching and overlap one end over the other by 1½ in / 3.8 cm. Trim the excess binding away and turn under a ¼ in / 0.6 cm seam on the short raw edges. Stitch across the start and finish points. Fold the binding over to the back of the project and slipstitch in place.

DOUBLE-FOLD BINDING

Double-fold binding provides a strong, solid edge and a more professional finish to quilts. Like single-fold binding it can be used for any width of binding and any fabric type. Fold the binding in half lengthways and press. Open out the binding. One at a time turn in each lengthways raw edge to the pressed center line, ensuring that there is no overlap. Press, then re-fold on the center line and press again. To attach the binding, follow the instructions for single-fold binding above.

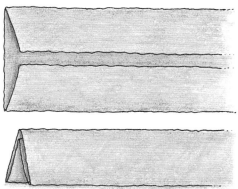

MITERED CORNERS USING SEPARATE BINDING

With right sides together center each border strip along each edge of the project so that a length of fabric overhangs each side. Work with one length at a time and baste to the pieced center with right sides together. Stitch each border to the pieced top to within ¼ in / 0.6 cm of the corner.

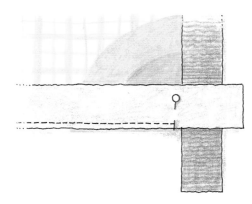

To miter the corners, overlap one piece of excess corner fabric over the other. Turn under the outer corner of the top piece of fabric at a 45° angle aligning it accurately with the strip underneath.

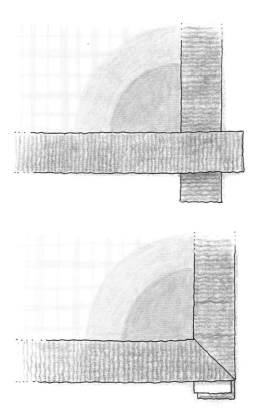

Press lightly, then slipstitch in place to secure. Trim away the excess fabric from underneath.

MITERED CORNERS USING CONTINUOUS BINDING

Prepare your length of binding following the instructions for either single- or double-fold binding. Refer to the pattern. Starting 6 in / 15.2 cm from the bottom left edge of the right side of the quilt, open out the folds of the binding and match one lengthways raw edge to the raw edge of the quilt top. Pin and baste in position. Stitch the binding through all the layers on the first pressed foldline of the binding. Continue until you reach ½ in / 1.3 cm

from the top left corner. To miter the corner, fold the binding strip away from the quilt top at a 45° angle. Hold the corner and fold the binding back adjacent with the quilt top. Pin. This fold will create a pleat allowing sufficient fabric to fold over the batting and backing and miter the corner. Stitch carefully around the edge of the corner.

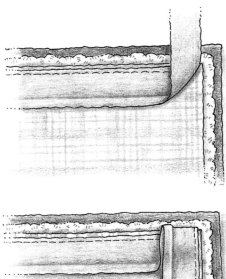

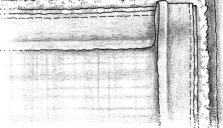

Continue stitching the binding to the square mitering each corner as you work. When you return to the start point, allow a 1 in / 2.5 cm overlap and turn under the raw edge on the short end of the binding. Fold the binding over to the back of the quilt so that it covers the stitching line of the front binding. Slipstitch in place, mitering the corners as you work.

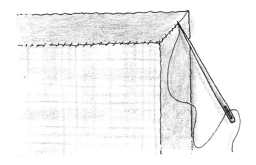

COVERING PIPING CORD

Measure the sides, top and bottom of your project and add to this measurement 12 in / 30.5 cm. Make continuous binding the length of your measurement × 1½ in / 3.8 cm wide. Fold the binding in half lengthways and press. Drop the cord into the fold of the binding and pin and baste in place. Using the zipper foot on the sewing machine and a co-ordinating thread, stitch very close to the cord so that it is tightly encased with the binding. Pin to the quilt top so that raw edges are aligned. At the point of overlap, undo the strands of the cord at each end and twist the ends together.

MAKING UP A CUSHION

For the back of the Old Oak Tree Cushion, the House Cushion, and the Nesting Hen Cushion, turn under ⅜ in / 1 cm on one long edge of the largest fabric piece. Turn under a further 1¼ in / 3.2 cm and press.

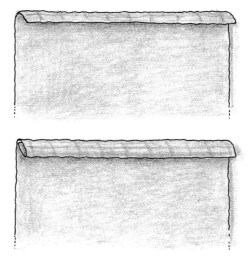

On the right side of the fabric, work a row of stitching close to the hemmed edge and a second row 1 in / 2.5 cm away. Repeat on one long edge of the

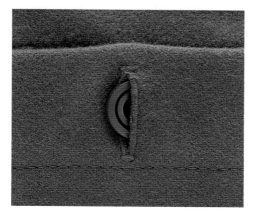

smaller length. Make three buttonholes equal distances apart on the hemmed edge of the larger piece.

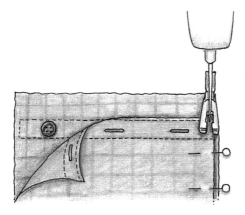

Stitch three buttons on the shorter piece to align with the buttonholes.

Spread out the pieces on a clean, flat surface. With right sides face up, overlap the hemmed edge of the larger piece over that of the small piece until the pieces together are the same size as the cushion front. Stitch together the overlap at each side.

With right sides facing, stitch the cushion front to the cushion back allowing ½ in / 1.3 cm seam. Turn right side out and insert the cushion pad into the cover.

BUTTONHOLES

Most modern sewing machines come complete with built-in buttonhole mechanisms. If you are working without one, it is possible to make buttonholes using the satin stitch or zigzag setting and altering the width. Work a sample buttonhole on a test piece of fabric first to ensure that the button will fit through the buttonhole.

Measure the length of your button and to this add ⅛ in / 0.3 cm. Using a colored thread make one large basting stitch the length of your measurement in the required position. Start at the top right-hand side of the basting stitch. Set the stitch width to 2 and the stitch length to between 0 and ½. Machine stitch down the right-hand side of the basting stitch. At the

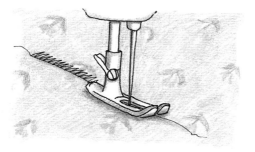

bottom stop and amend the stitch width to 4. Stitch a bar of four or five stitches. Lift the presser foot and turn the fabric around 180°. Set the stitch width to 2 and satin stitch down the other side of the basting stitch. At the end, set the stitch width to 4 and stitch a bar across to secure each end. Remove the basting stitch and slit the buttonhole.

STITCH GLOSSARY

Use the illustrations below as a guide. If you are a novice stitcher, practice a few stitches first on a sample piece of fabric. Make all your stitches the same length and keep an even tension throughout. Use an embroidery hoop for ease of stitching.

Stem stitch

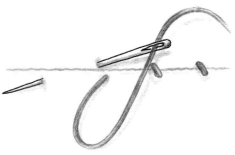

Slipstitch

Running stitch

French knot

Back stitch

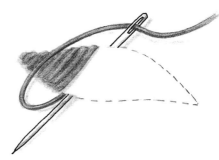

Satin stitch

Chain stitch

Stab stitch

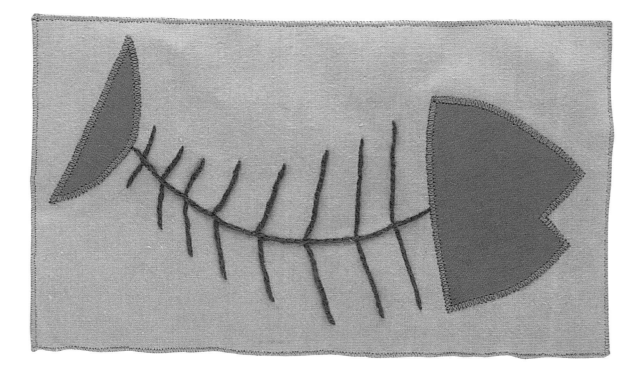

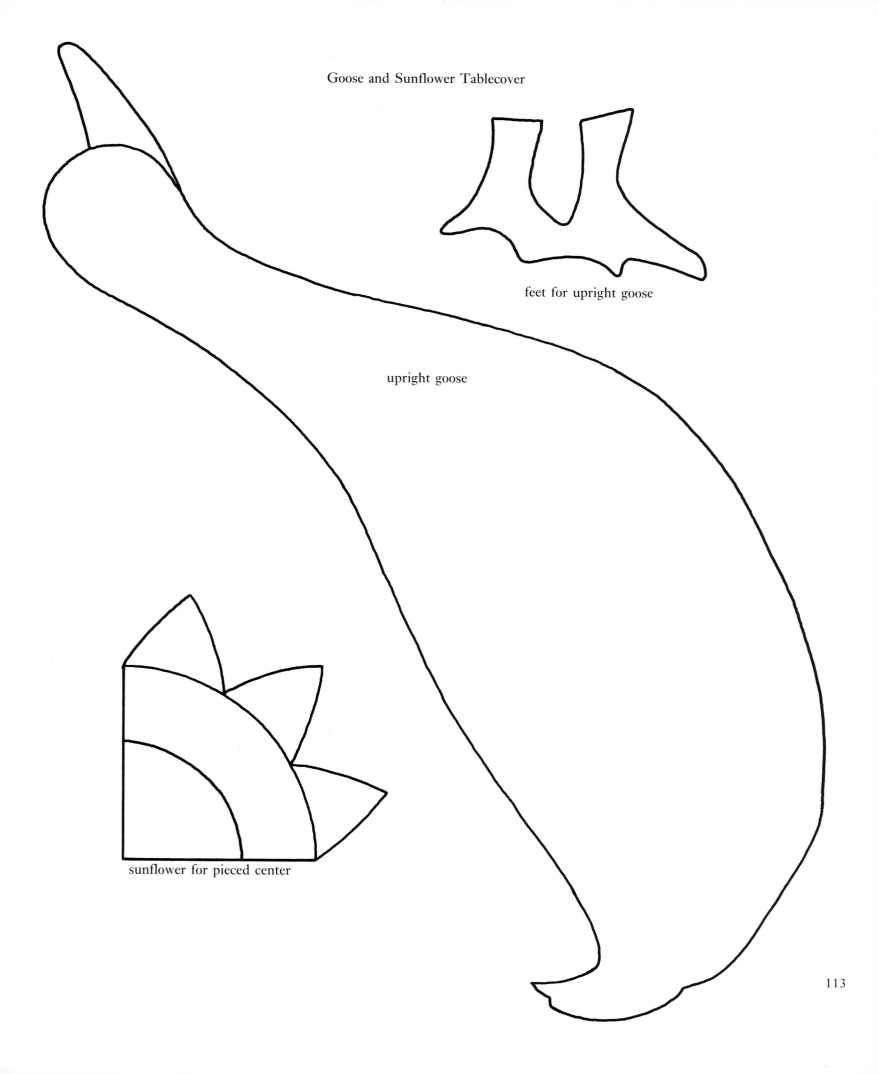

Goose and Sunflower Tablecover

feet for upright goose

upright goose

sunflower for pieced center

113

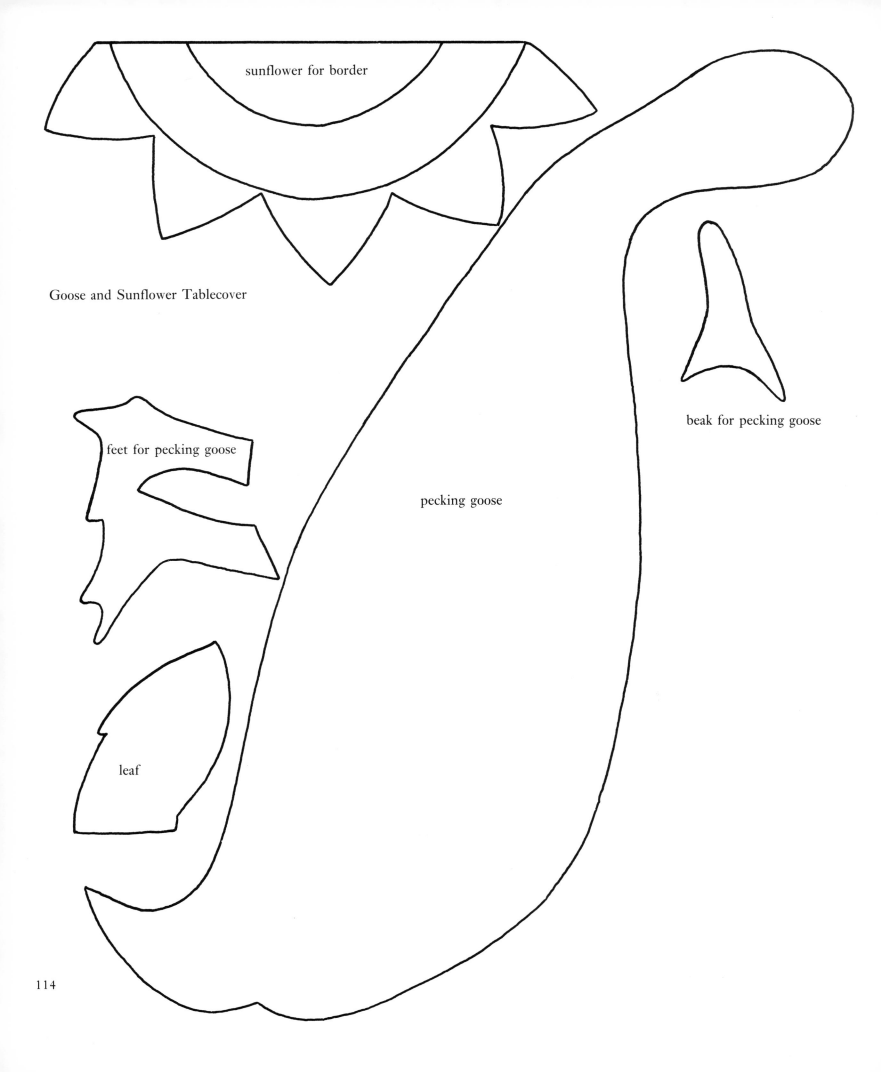

sunflower for border

Goose and Sunflower Tablecover

beak for pecking goose

feet for pecking goose

pecking goose

leaf

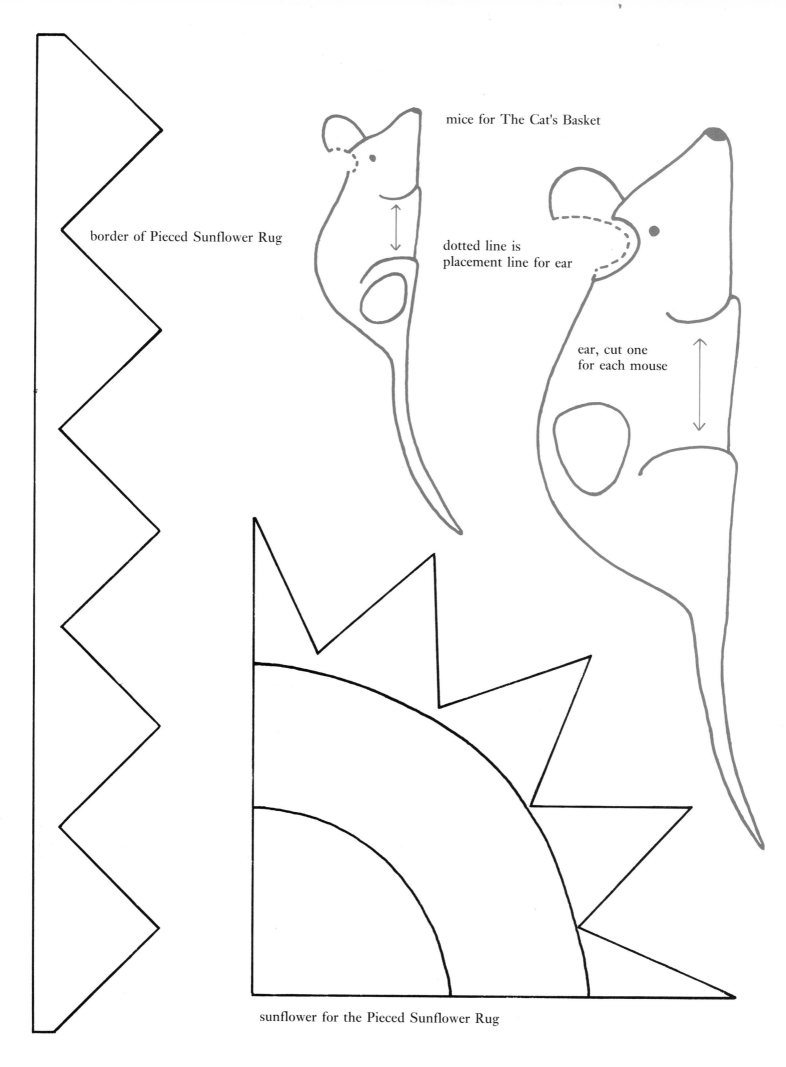

border of Pieced Sunflower Rug

mice for The Cat's Basket

dotted line is
placement line for ear

ear, cut one
for each mouse

sunflower for the Pieced Sunflower Rug

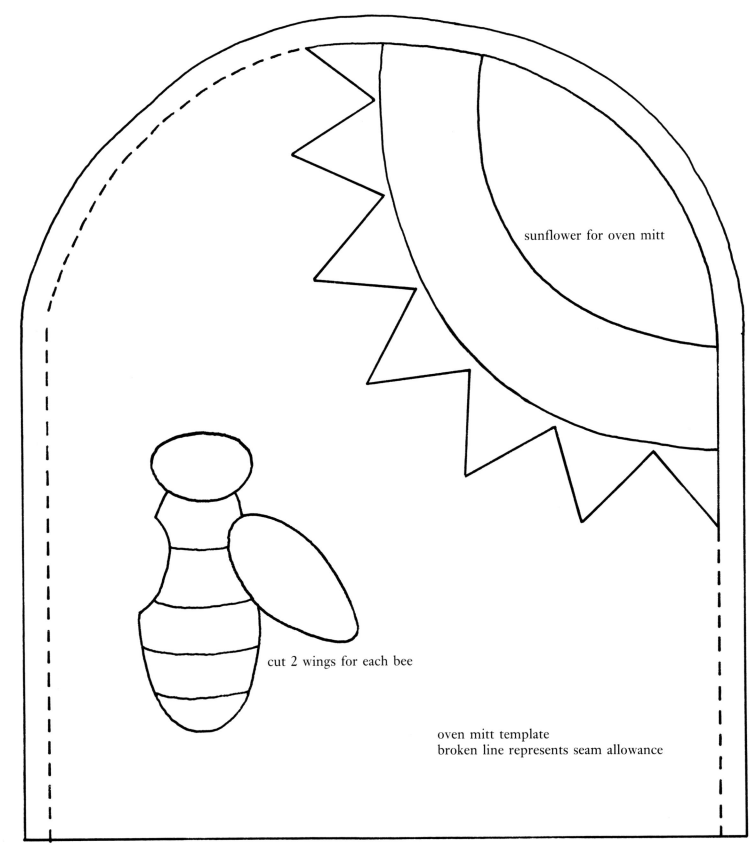

sunflower for oven mitt

cut 2 wings for each bee

oven mitt template
broken line represents seam allowance

Nesting Hen Cushion

G

E

H

D

C

F

enlarge to 10½ in / 26.7 cm

117

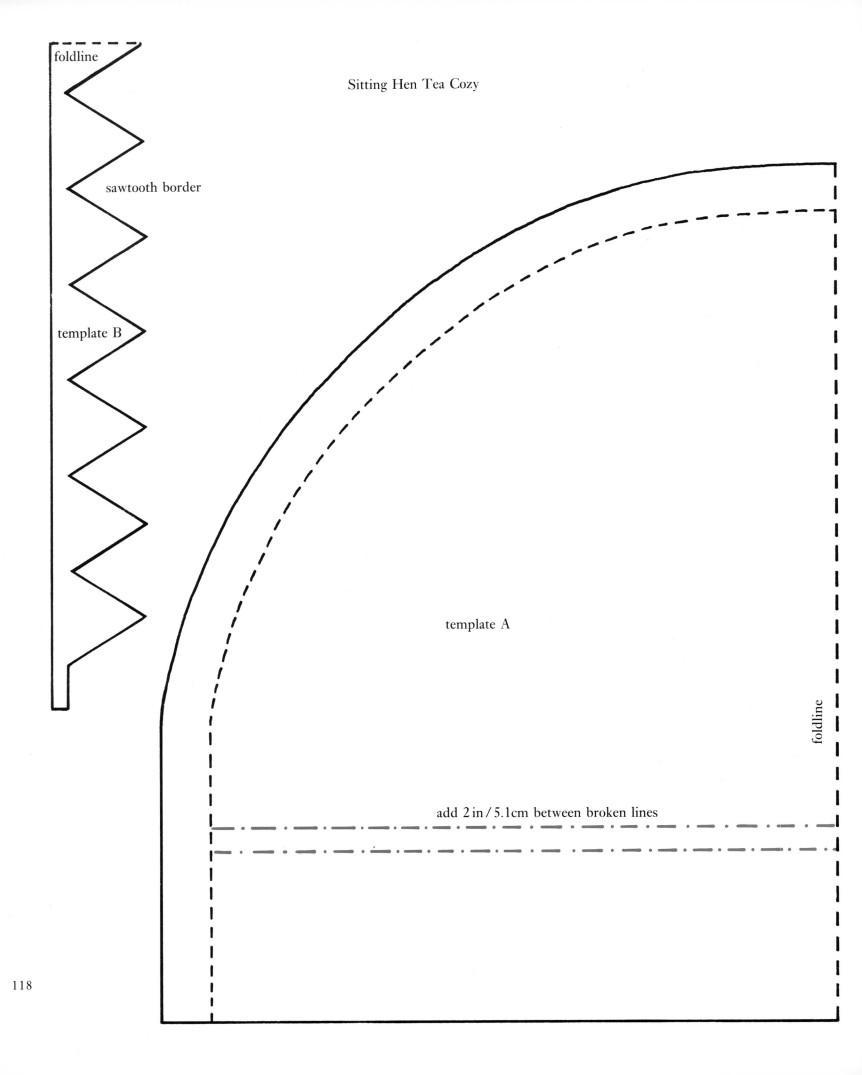

foldline

Sitting Hen Tea Cozy

sawtooth border

template B

template A

foldline

add 2 in / 5.1 cm between broken lines

Sitting Hen Tea Cozy

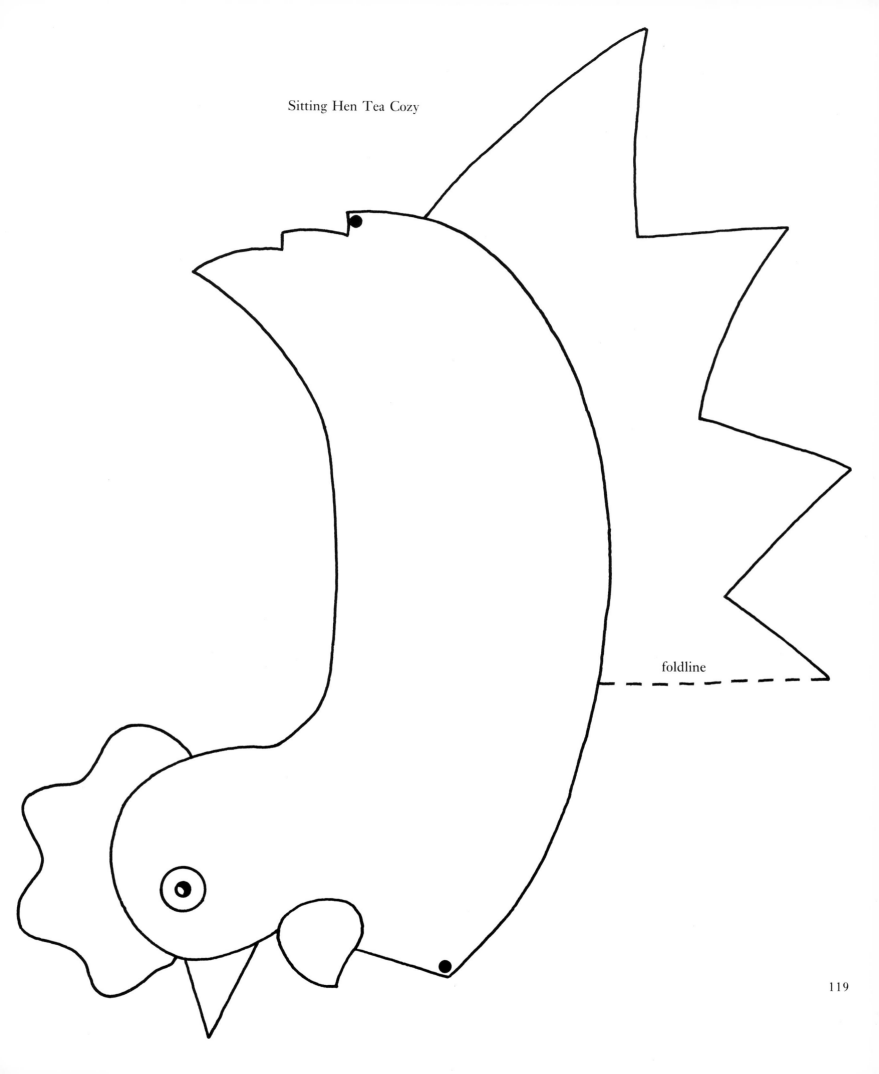

foldline

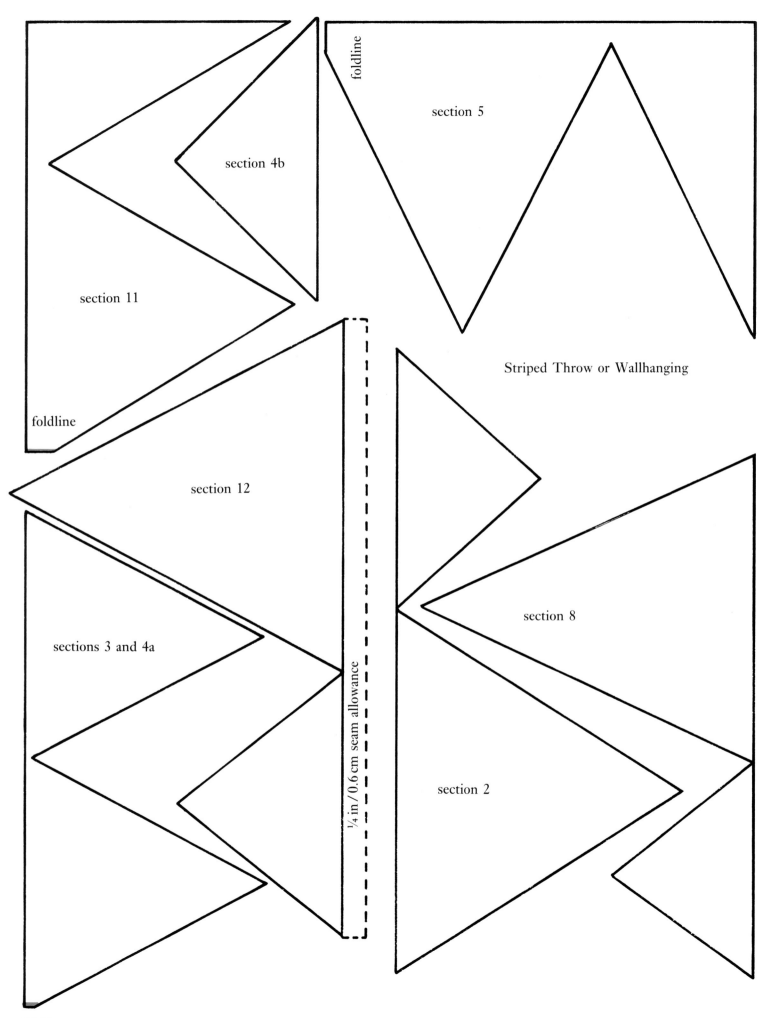

section 5

section 4b

section 11

foldline

foldline

Striped Throw or Wallhanging

section 12

section 8

sections 3 and 4a

¼ in / 0.6 cm seam allowance

section 2

foldline

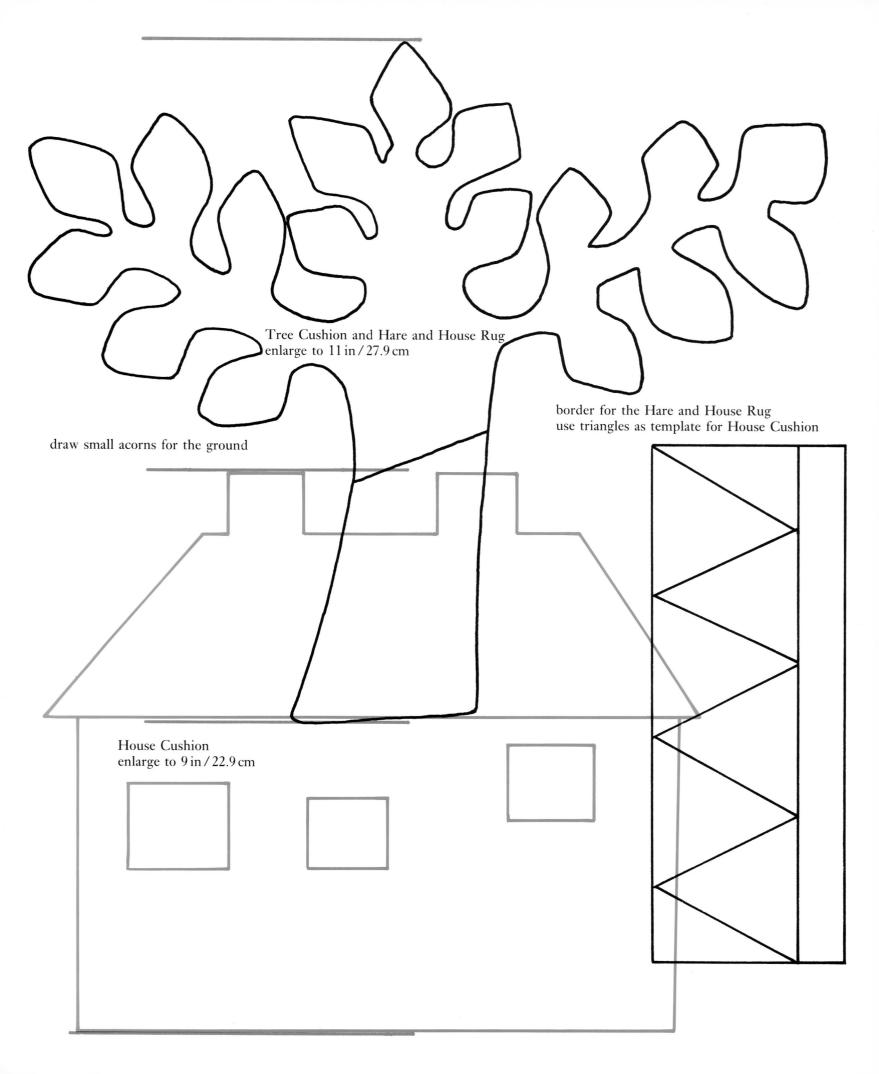

Tree Cushion and Hare and House Rug
enlarge to 11 in / 27.9 cm

draw small acorns for the ground

border for the Hare and House Rug
use triangles as template for House Cushion

House Cushion
enlarge to 9 in / 22.9 cm

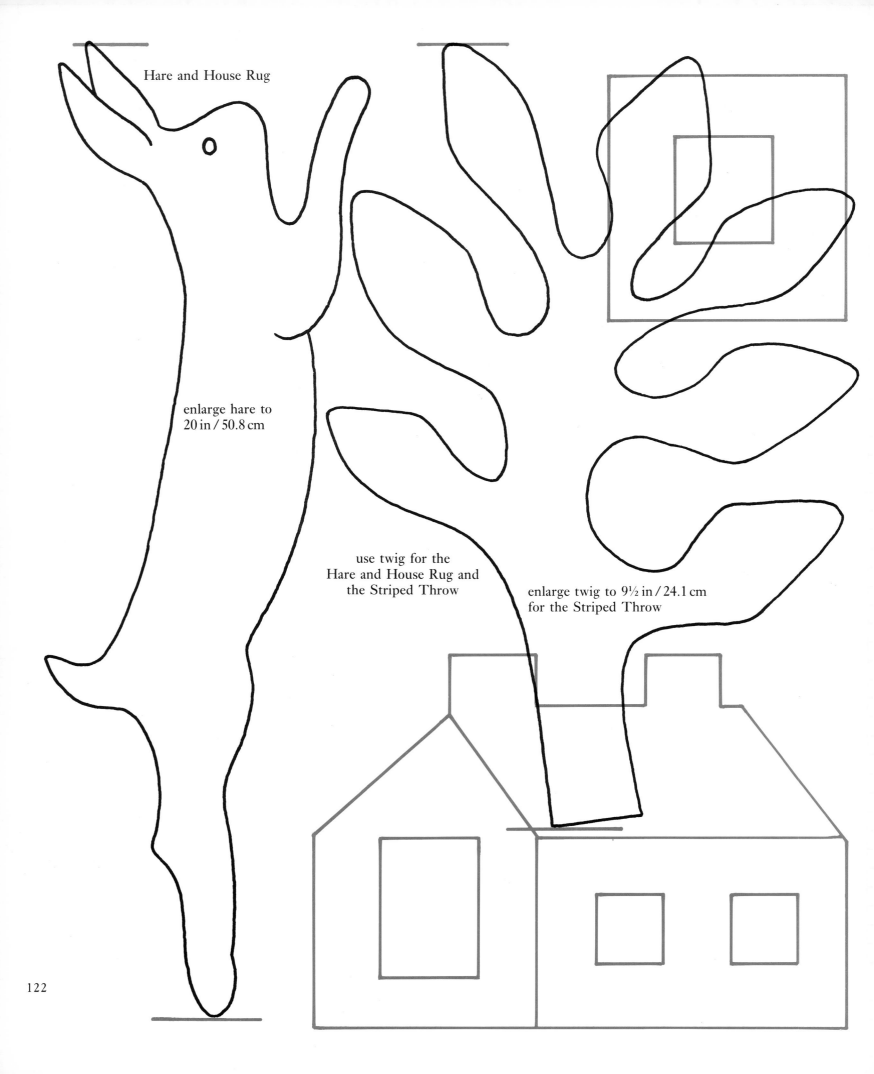

Hare and House Rug

enlarge hare to
20 in / 50.8 cm

use twig for the
Hare and House Rug and
the Striped Throw

enlarge twig to 9½ in / 24.1 cm
for the Striped Throw

122

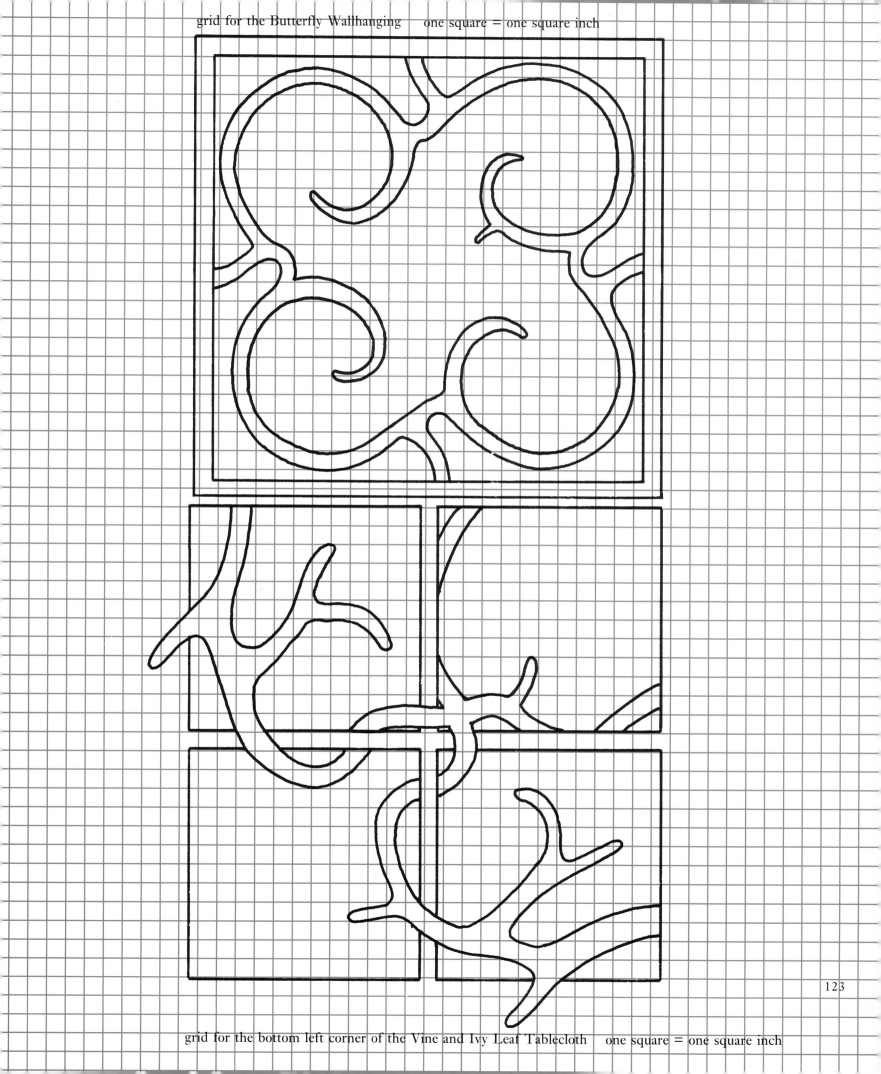

grid for the Butterfly Wallhanging   one square = one square inch

123

grid for the bottom left corner of the Vine and Ivy Leaf Tablecloth   one square = one square inch

Vine and Ivy Leaf Tablecloth

broken line represents vine position

124

use for Vine and Ivy Leaf Tablecloth and the Flower Cushion

125

Butterfly Wallhanging

enlarge snail to 9¼ in / 24 cm long for the
Vine and Ivy Leaf Tablecloth

Butterfly Wallhanging

enlarge flower to 7¼ in / 18.4 cm
for Vine and Ivy Leaf Tablecloth
enlarge bee to 4¾ in / 12.2 cm long
for Vine and Ivy Leaf Tablecloth

broken line represents
position of stem

127

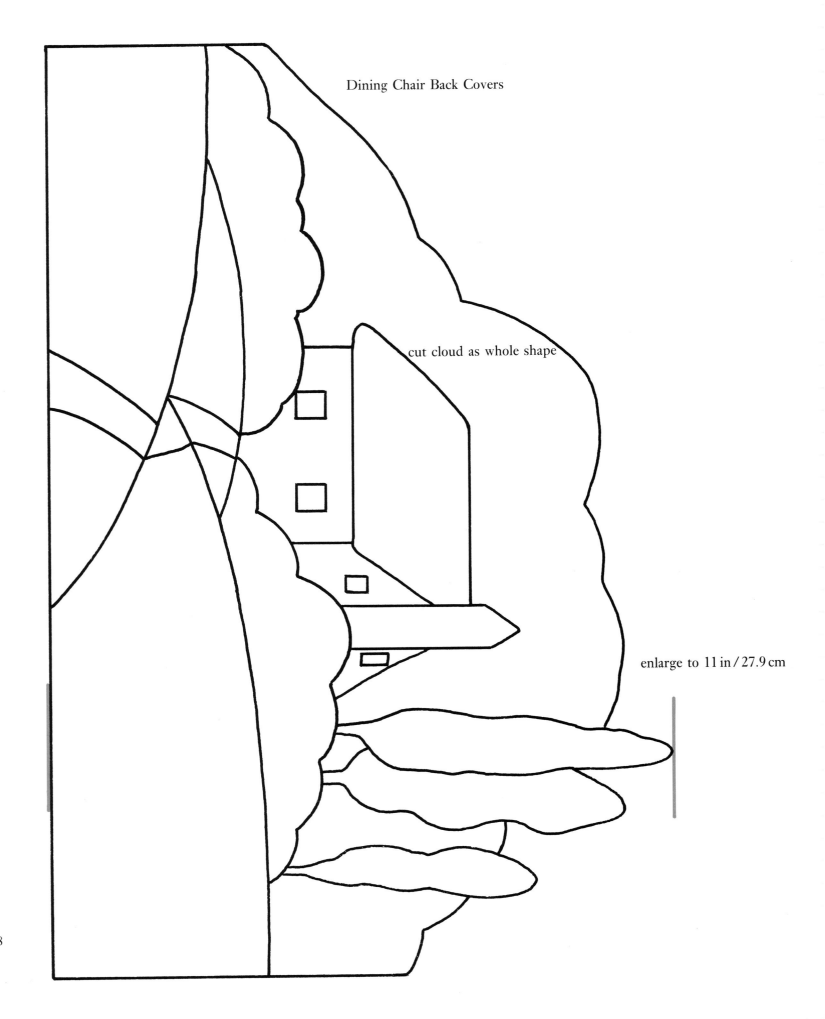

Dining Chair Back Covers

cut cloud as whole shape

enlarge to 11 in / 27.9 cm

128

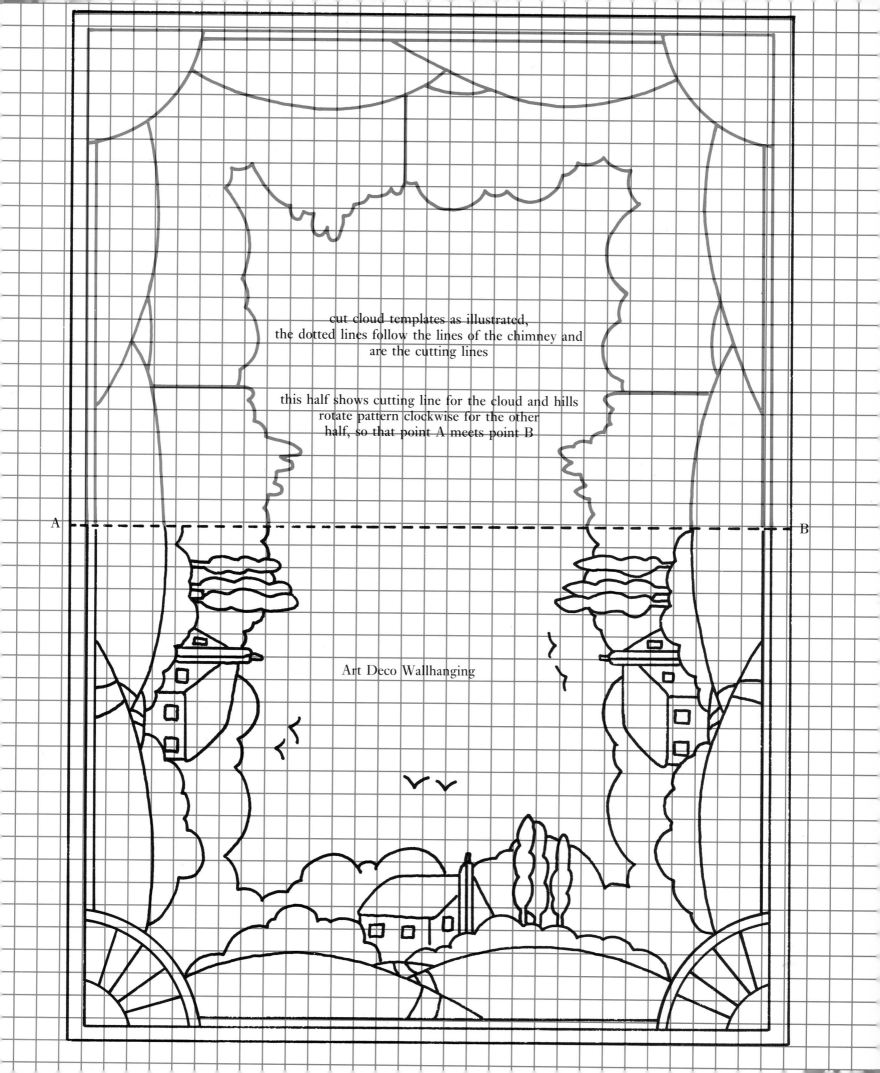

cut cloud templates as illustrated,
the dotted lines follow the lines of the chimney and
are the cutting lines

this half shows cutting line for the cloud and hills
rotate pattern clockwise for the other
half, so that point A meets point B

A — — — — — — — — — — — — — — — — — — — B

Art Deco Wallhanging

Clarice Cliff Drapes

left-hand drape of a pair, reverse pattern for the right-hand drape

enlarge letters to fit pocket

Contented Cat Quilt

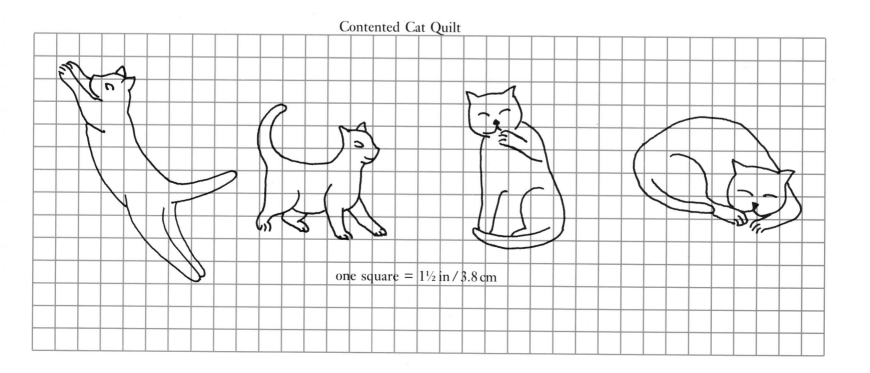

one square = 1½ in / 3.8 cm

Contented Cat Quilt

B

A

A

B

C

C

B

A

pocket flap liner

leaf

Contented Cat Quilt

E
D
C

A B C D E F G H J K L

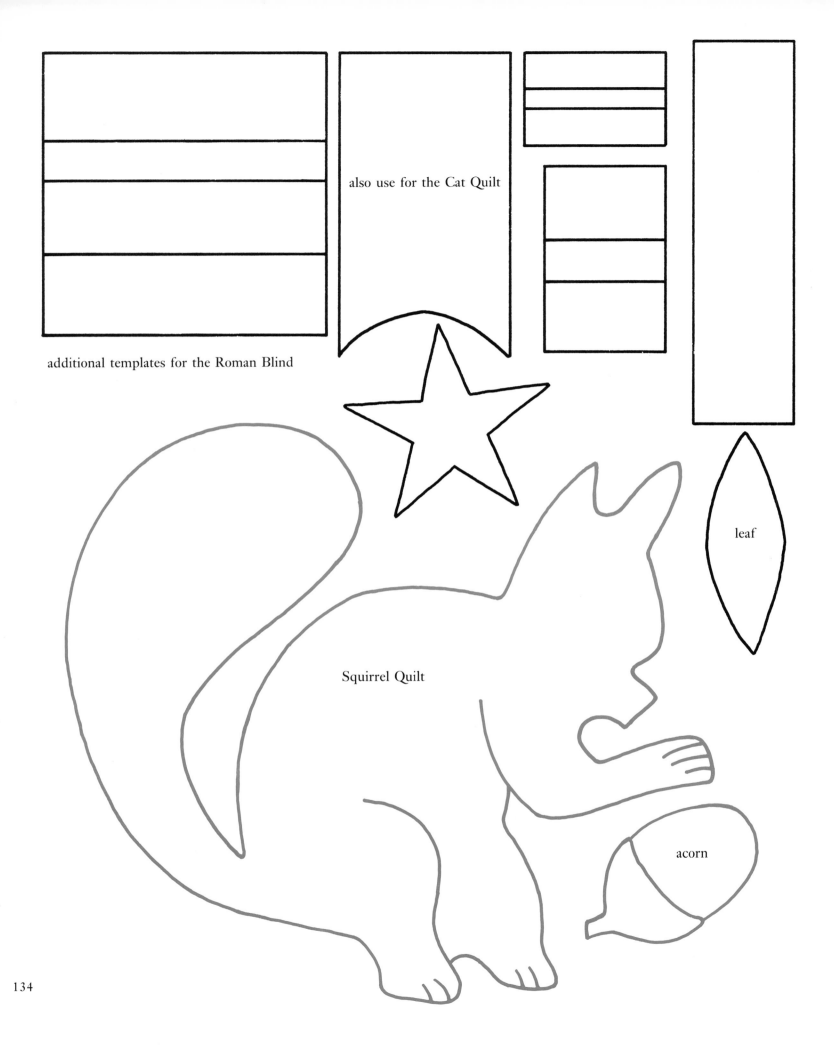

also use for the Cat Quilt

additional templates for the Roman Blind

leaf

Squirrel Quilt

acorn

134

cowboy for Bolster Cushion

tree for Squirrel Quilt

use tree for Toybox, Cowboy Rug and Bolster Cushion

135

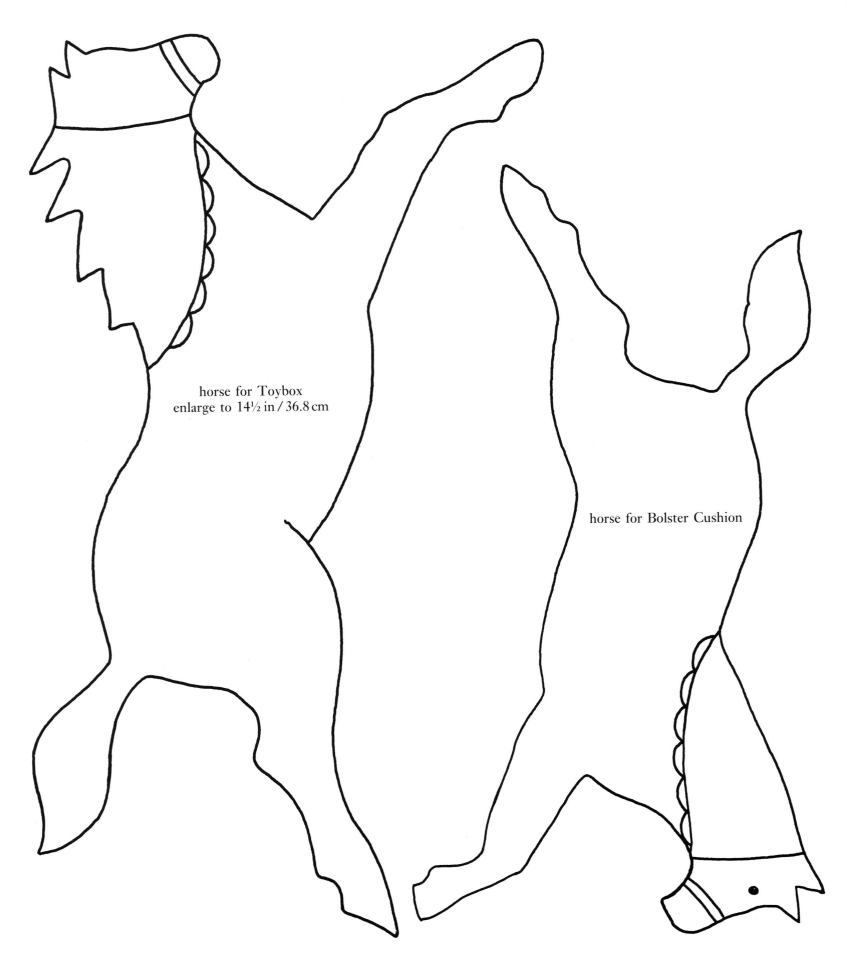

horse for Toybox
enlarge to 14½ in / 36.8 cm

horse for Bolster Cushion

136

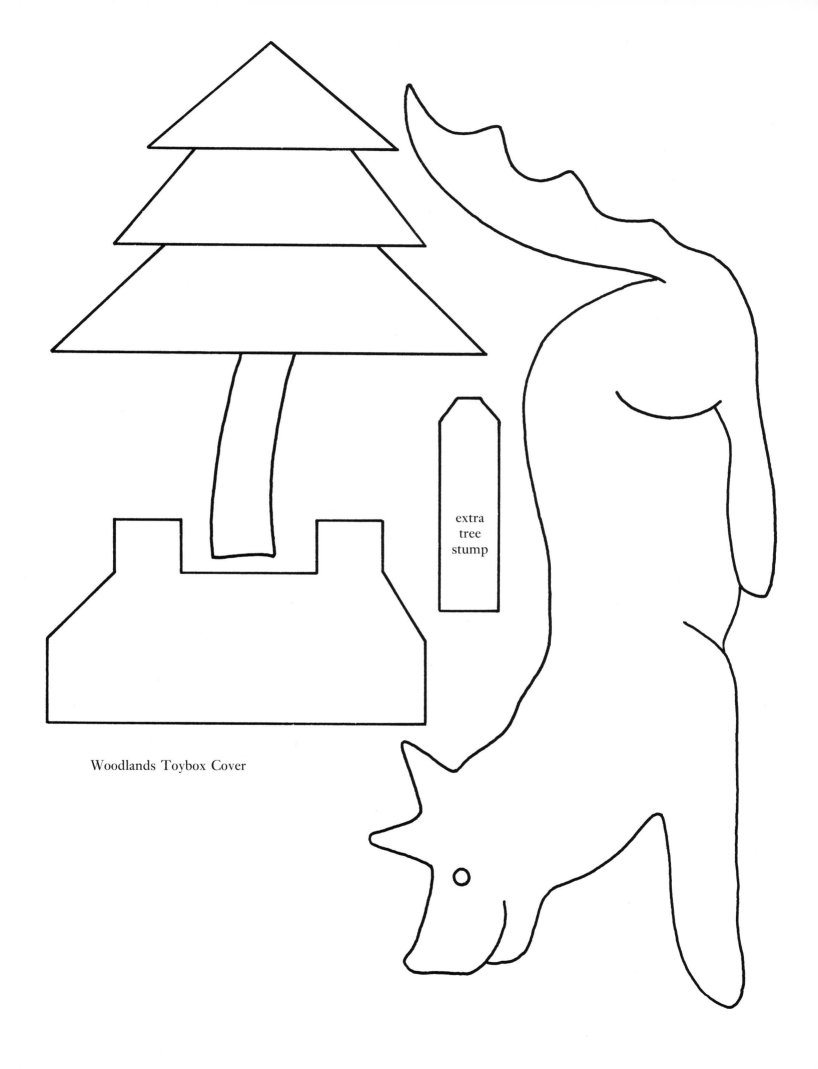

Woodlands Toybox Cover

extra
tree
stump

Cowboy for Toybox

use the tree for the Bolster Cushion,
Toybox and Cowboy Rug

138

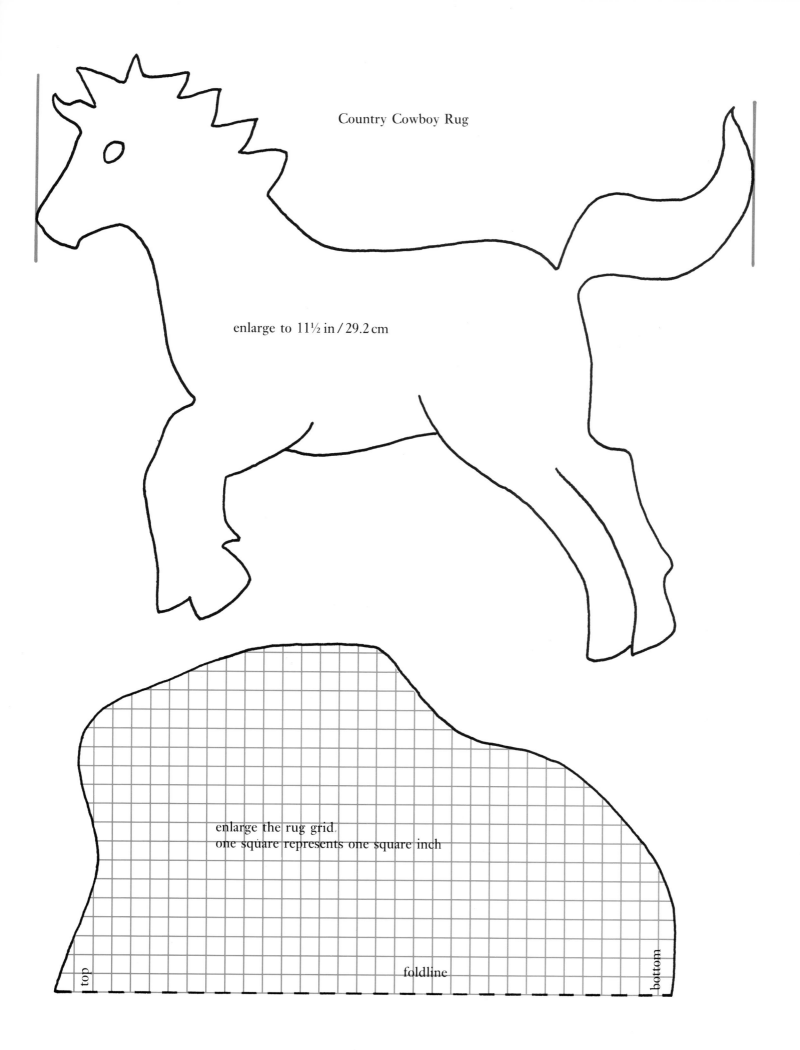

Country Cowboy Rug

enlarge to 11½ in / 29.2 cm

enlarge the rug grid.
one square represents one square inch

top

foldline

bottom

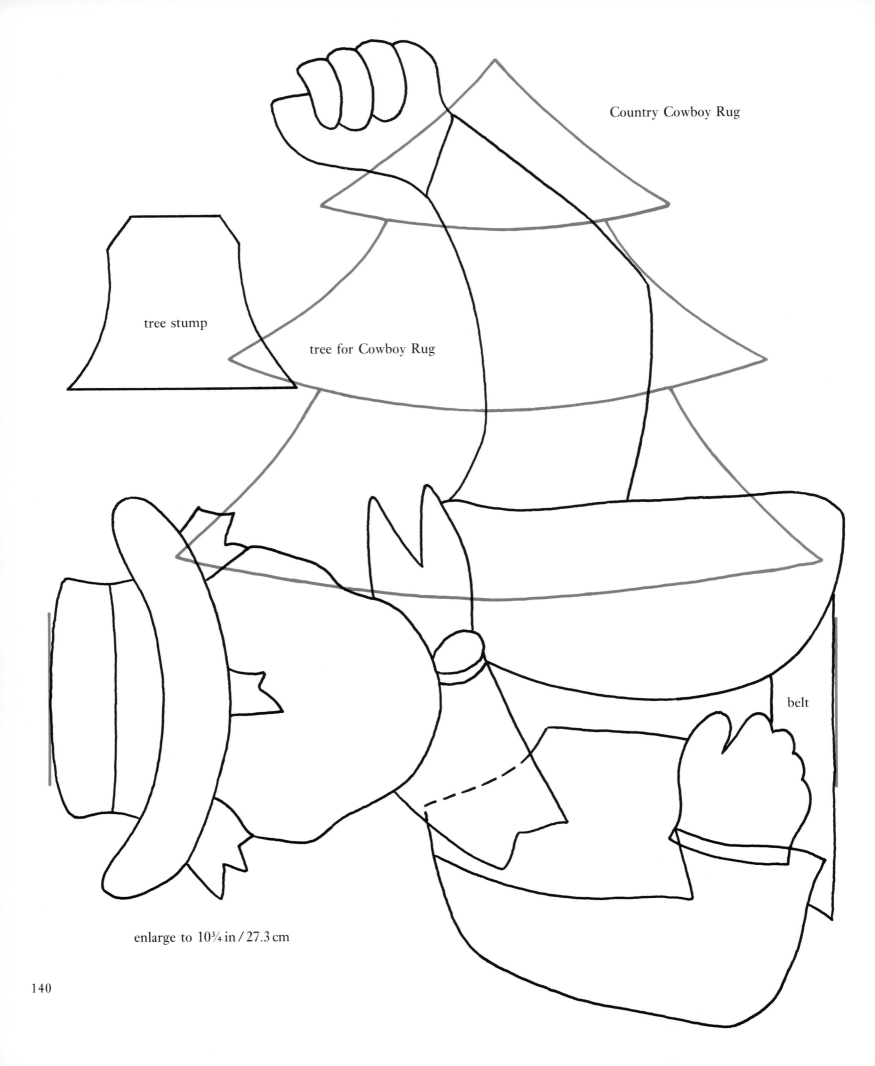

Country Cowboy Rug

tree stump

tree for Cowboy Rug

belt

enlarge to 10¾ in / 27.3 cm

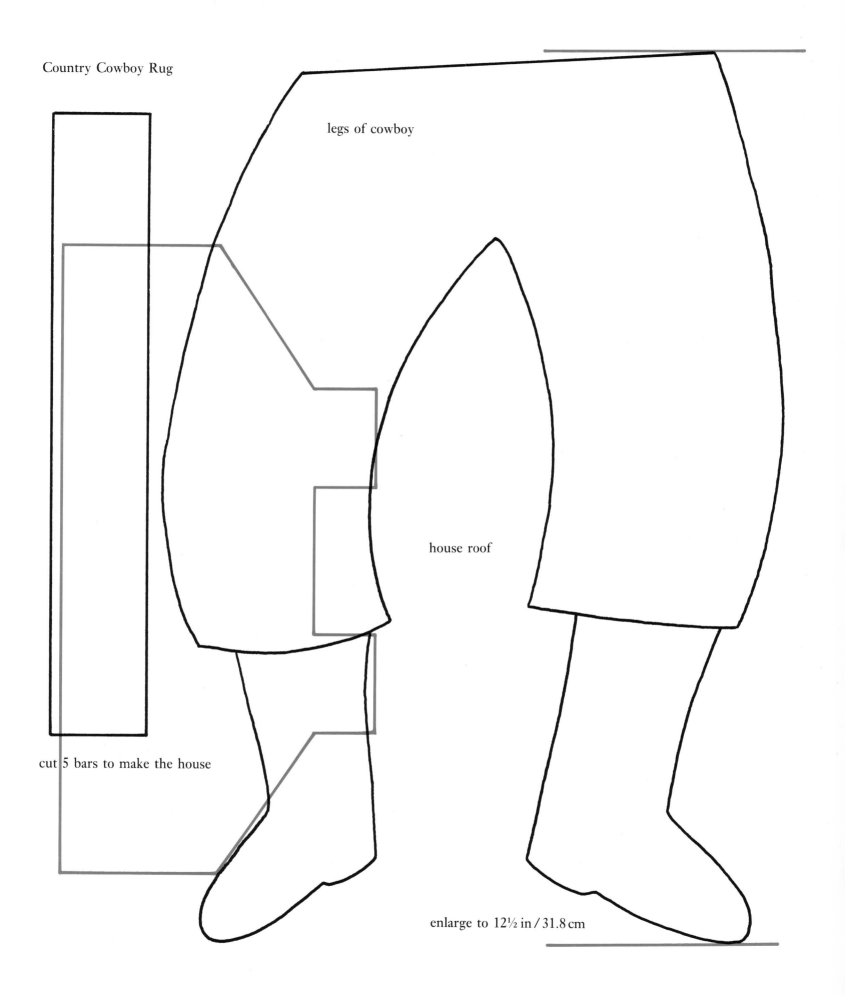

Country Cowboy Rug

legs of cowboy

cut 5 bars to make the house

house roof

enlarge to 12½ in / 31.8 cm

INDEX

ACKNOWLEDGEMENTS

Many thanks are due to Marcus Brothers Textiles, Inc, 1460 Broadway, New York, NY 10036, USA, for supplying the wonderful cotton flannels used to make many of the projects in this book.

It has been my good fortune to work with many highly talented and skilled people at Museum Quilts Publications. I am indebted to the entire staff, who, despite their own hectic schedules and professional demands, always seem available for help and advice. Annlee Landman and Caroline Wilkinson came to my rescue when it appeared that two of the projects could not be finished on time. I have enjoyed working with my co-author, Carol Hart. Together we shared the despair of tight schedules and seemingly impossible deadlines and together we heaved a sigh of satisfaction when everything was finally finished. A special thank you to my husband, Denis, who cleared the decks to help me and put up with fabric, needles and pins covering every square inch of our home.

Adele Corcoran

Thanks to my editors, my co-author Adele Corcoran, my husband Barry and my family for their enthusiasm and interest.

Carol Hart